Stéphanie Dreuillet

UNUSUAL HOTELS
FRANCE

JONGLEZ

NOTE FROM THE PUBLISHER

Over the years, we have become more and more selective in choosing the hotels where we spend our vacations or weekends.

Without even mentioning chain hotels, finding a "charming" hotel is often difficult, all the more so as the standards of certain ratings often seem insufficient.

Here, it is not a question of price, as some expensive luxury hotels are also to be avoided because of exaggerated prices, complacent or impersonal service, and sometimes unstylish architecture.

It is, however, a question of character, quality of service, and accommodation. We have seen too many hotels that were aesthetically perfect in a brochure but where deplorable treatment ruined the trip.

All of these elements left us wanting more. In addition to the key essentials, we wanted a place that surprised us, that had something we wouldn't find anywhere else: uncommon architecture, a unique concept, an original geographic location.

Of course, our list of uncommon hotels, B&Bs and self-catering cottages isn't exhaustive. Some places, although uncommon, didn't live up to our expectations due to their architecture, décor, surroundings or service.

I hope our selection will meet your expectations.

Thomas Jonglez

Note: We refuse to accept any financial compensation for mentioning hotels and sites in our guidebooks.

Send us your suggestions

Comments about this guidebook and its contents, as well as information about sites not mentioned here, are welcome. They will serve to enrich our future editions.

Please write us at:

Jonglez Publishing, 17, boulevard du Roi, 78000 Versailles, France

E-mail: info@jonglezpublishing.com

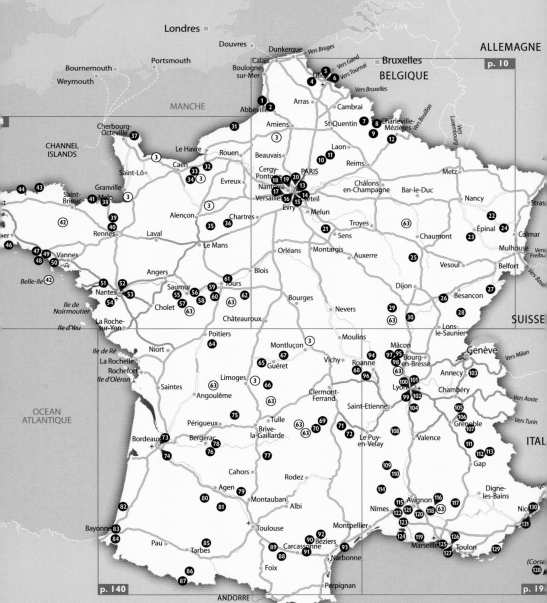

INDEX

NORTH, EAST AND ILE DE FRANCE

WEST

SOUTHWEST

INDEX

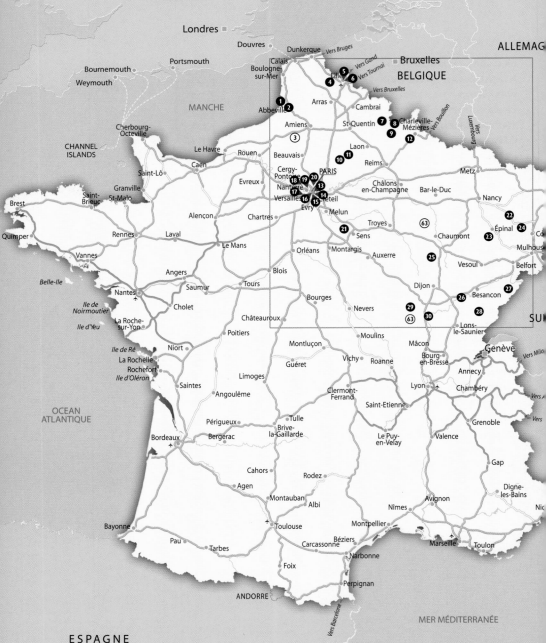

NORTH, EAST & ILE DE FRANCE

LE BRUIT DE L'EAU (THE SOUND OF WATER)

Sleep in a Zen dojo on a private island

LE BRUIT DE L'EAU ❶
80120 Saint-Quentin-
en-Tourmont
Tel. 06 08 62 88 84
www.lebruitdeleau.org
contact@lebruitdeleau.org

ROOMS AND RATES
3 rooms and 1 dojo
Different packages
beginning at 228€
for 2 people
including breakfast,
private access to the spa,
and culinary discoveries
Rituals starting at
75€ per person
Rooms open year round
"After the Rain" suite
open from the first
day of spring to
the last day of autumn

In Japan, a ryokan is a traditional inn where guests who have come to spend the night are paid the utmost attention. Meals are often served in the room, and the small interior garden present in most ryokans provides a feeling of calm and relaxation.

It is from this tradition that Tibo and his wife drew their inspiration to create this ecological and heavenly place located at the heart of the Somme region, near the Parc du Marquenterre. The 2.5-acre garden at the centre of the property is home to a butterfly garden, beehives and a dragonfly garden, all of which are managed in collaboration with various local associations.

A traditional dojo (a place for Zen meditation) has also been built on a small private island. It is only open in the summer, however, as its walls are made of paper.

All of the rooms are equipped with tatamis and futons. The spa is exclusively wood-heated and invites guests to discover the Siberian banya (a Russian sauna where one uses tree branches to lightly lash one's body), the Finnish sauna, or the Furo-Oké (Japanese bath).

A rare site.

HUTTE DES 400 COUPS

A hunting lodge camouflaged in nature

HUTTE DES 400 COUPS ❷
80860 Sailly-Bray
Tel. 03 22 60 24 24
www.baiedesomme.fr
hutte.400coups@
baiedesomme.fr

ROOMS AND RATES
Open year round
March to July:
170€ a night
for 1 to 4 people
3-night package: 460€
290€ a night
for 5 to 7 people
3-night package: 680€
August to January: hunting
package (special rates)

It was in 1904 that Viscount Henri Brossin de Méré, an avid waterfowl hunter, had this lodge built for his hunting pleasure in this Sailly-Bray marsh.

Designed to blend in fully with its surroundings, the lodge is perfectly camouflaged and allows guests to observe a multitude of migrating birds as they pass through the region.

The "400 Coups" lodge (whose name supposedly comes from the 400-shot salute fired as a prelude to the inaugural dinner the Viscount held at the time) offers surprising comfort and a unique atmosphere. Whereas most hunting lodges were rather sparsely furnished, the Viscount's lodge had a firing range, bedrooms, a dining-room, kitchen, lavatory, kennel, workroom, gunroom, storage, showers, a shelter, and the "Viscountess's chambers".

Today, the lodge remains a lovely little house facing a 5-acre pond in the middle of nature.

UN LIT AU PRÉ®

"Where overworked city dwellers live like Robinson Crusoe."

UN LIT AU PRÉ® ③
Côte de Nacre (Calvados),
Pays d'Auge (Calvados),
Baie du Mont-Saint-
Michel (Manche),
Portes du Perche
(Orne), Vallée des
Evoissons (Picardy),
Plateau de Millevaches
(Haute-Vienne)
and Auvergne (Allier).
Other farms welcome
"Un Lit au Pré®" every year
Contact: Guillaume Wibaux
Tel. 01 41 31 08 00
www.unlitaupre.fr
info@unlitaupre.fr

ROOMS AND RATES
6-person tents
(maximum 5 adults)
Weekend (Friday 4pm
to Monday 10.30am):
from 255€ to 425€
depending on the season
Easter weekend: 435€
Pentecost weekend: 495€
Weekend of the Ascension
(5 nights): 595€
Mid-week: Monday to
Friday: from 205€ to 515€
Full week: Friday to
Friday: from 414€ to 835€
depending on the season
Open from Easter to
All Saints' Day

Guillaume Wibaux is a passionate man. His numerous travels, constant contact with locals, love of beautiful scenery, and desire to get back to the basics, even for a few days, encouraged him to adopt a concept that is highly popular in England and the Netherlands. That was how "Un Lit au Pré®" (A Bed in the Meadow) was born in 2008.

This carefully designed concept allows a family (up to 6 people) to share a farmer's life while remaining independent and spending a few days in a beautiful and comfortable tent. These 45m² tents, which are all identical, were designed especially for "Un Lit au Pré®". They include a living-room, a "guest-room" with bunk beds, a master bedroom, and an incredible box-bed large enough to hold 1 or 2 children. The front part of the tent can open up to create an outdoor living space.

A woodstove, the showpiece of the tent, stands in the centre of the living-room. It serves to heat the tent, but also for cooking. Here, you'll find no television, computer or electricity, just the sounds of nature – those of the animals and farmers.

With help from the farmers, the children take part in feeding and milking the animals, and, if they're lucky, they'll witness an animal birth. The farms are chosen in a very selective manner in favour of farmers who have a strong desire to share their lifestyle and who show true generosity. Each farm has a storeroom where the family can find food staples: products from the farm or neighbouring farms. Here, the owners don't provide a prepared breakfast, but you'll find fresh milk, eggs, and bread baked fresh in an on-site bread oven. On the farm, the children are treated like kings: bike-rides, games of hide-and-seek in the hay, or a nightly stroll to admire the stars after an evening spent playing games or reading by candlelight.

The Pouzieux estate, in Auvergne, is exclusively equipped with the "Spa au Pré" (Spa in the Meadow), an outdoor wooden bath heated by wood that is left at the visitor's disposal.

GUEST COMMENTS

"A magnificent and unforgettable stay, notably thanks to the kindness and availability of our host farmers."

LA GARE DES ANNÉES FOLLES
(THE ROARING TWENTIES TRAIN STATION)

The only PLM train car in France turned into a hotel

LA GARE DES ANNÉES FOLLES ❹
77, rue de la Gare
62840 Sailly-sur-la-Lys
Tel. 03 21 02 68 20
www.lagaredesanneesfolles.fr
chefdegare@
lagaredesanneesfolles.fr

ROOMS AND RATES
7 compartments, 2 showers
and 2 lavatories, parlour,
garden and terrace
1-person compartment: 39€
2-person compartment
(bunk beds): 49€
2 one-person compartments
with connecting door: 69€
Nuptual suite
(double bed): 89€
Breakfast: 6.50€
To reserve
the entire car: 350€
Restaurant open daily,
closed Sunday evenings
and Mondays
Open year round

There are only 2 PLM train cars remaining in France: one is at the railway museum in Mulhouse, and the other near the former Bac Saint-Maur railway station. It is in this old 1930 train car, with its original mahogany and sycamore woodwork with mother-of-pearl accents, that 7 guest-rooms were professionally installed and renovated. Only the showers are new.

Acquired by the SNCF (French national railway company) in 1938, this sleeping-car, along with 12 others that once made up the train, was pulled by a steam engine and connected Paris to Lyon and the Mediterranean, making for a very luxurious overnight trip.

Today, the compartments can accommodate 1 or 2 people on bunk-beds; the former restaurant area at the end of the car has been transformed into a nuptial suite with a double bed.

Breakfast is served in the adjacent railway station which, thanks to its luggage racks and bottle-green-coloured seat cushions, has retained its original ambience. The décor of the waiting area and restaurant has been entirely redone in Art Deco style: pearl chandeliers, unmatched porcelain dishes, an old clock and antique books.

Truly a trip back in time.

LA MAISON CARRÉE

For the love of art

LA MAISON CARRÉE ❺
29, rue Bonte Pollet
59000 Lille
Tel. 03 20 93 60 42
www.lamaisoncarree.fr
reservation@
lamaisoncarree.fr

ROOMS AND RATES
3 rooms, from 140€
to 160€ for 1 or 2 people,
breakfast included
2 suites, 230€ for 2 people
One of the suites is a duplex
including a guest-room
with a double bed and
stairs leading to another
room with 2 single beds:
270€ a night for 4 people,
breakfast included

Hidden behind high walls, the Maison Carrée (Square House) is a former private mansion dating from the early 20th century that has been converted into a B&B and conference centre.

Its originality lies in its magnificent contemporary art collection (paintings, sculptures, photos) that is displayed throughout the house and which blends subtly with the house's older elements.

The collection includes works by Nan Goldin, Alicia Paz, Roland Fischer and Victor Rodriguez, to name a few — a truly private small museum.

The Maison Carrée has 3 guest-rooms and 2 charming suites that offer the same amenities as the best hotels (bathrobe, slippers and fine beauty products). Breakfast is served on fine china among the masterpieces hanging in the large dining-room.

Adding to the B&B's charm is its large garden with a terrace in exotic woods, and a swimming pool.

> The mansion, which now hosts contemporary art exhibits year round, is also open to interested visitors.

THE "LILLE FLOTTANTE" BARGE

Sleep on a barge just steps away from Lille's city centre

PÉNICHE LILLE FLOTTANTE ❻
Square du Ramponneau
Champ de Mars
59000 Lille
Tel. 03 20 07 92 38
or 06 30 39 14 06
www.lilleflottante.com
bienvenue@lilleflottante.com

ROOMS AND RATES
2 cabins
165€ for 2 people,
breakfast included
On-site parking
Flat-screen TVs
Internet access
Adjustable beds
Massage showers
Bathrobes and slippers
Baby-sitting, board games
and toys for children,
baby equipment available,
Thaï massages
Open year round

Docked across from Ramponneau Square at the entrance to the Bois de Boulogne and Vauban's Citadel, near Lille's Old City, the "Lille Flottante" barge is a "Freyssinet" barge (38.5m long and 5m wide) that invites you aboard.

The two bedrooms overlook the water, allowing guests to admire ducks and herons as they peacefully paddle along. The bargee's quarters, at the back of the boat, were once occupied by the boatman and his family, where the captain's helm is located. It still has its original portholes and can accommodate a family with 2 young children. At this B&B far from the noise of the city yet quite close to the city centre, the hostess welcomes guests in a friendly, discreet manner.

Opening onto the parlour, the library, with its cushions, ottomans and sofas, invites guests to sit down and thumb through the numerous books about the ocean and barges.

THE FORMER LOCK HOUSES OF THIÉRACHE

The tranquility of the countryside along a boat-towing route

THE FORMER LOCK HOUSES OF THIÉRACHE ❼
Les Roseaux 02120 Tupigny
La Reinette 02510 Hannapes
Les Rayères 02120
Lesquielles-Saint-Germain
Contact: Demeures
de Thiérache
Tel. 06 77 99 97 67
www.demeuresdethierache.com
demeuresdethierache@initialite.com

ROOMS AND RATES
Les Roseaux:
weekend rate from 213€,
week rate from 281€
(2 rooms for 3 to 5 people)
La Reinette:
weekend rate from 191€,
week rate from 265€
(3 rooms for 6 people)
Les Rayères:
weekend rate from 215€,
week rate from 322€
(3 rooms for 6 people)

"Demeures de Thiérache" is an association founded in 1995 to manage the rental of certain residences in the Thiérache region. Among these residences are three lock houses owned by Voies Navigables de France (French Navigable Waterways) which have been renovated and turned into self-catering cottages.

Located on the Sambre à l'Oise canal, these old houses are perfect for fishing trips and to enjoy the calm countryside along this boat-towing route.

The first two houses, which each have an enclosed garden, are close to each another. The last house, called "Les Rayères", bears the name of the small waterfall where the Oise River splits into two branches. This waterfall flows at the base of a window of one of the bedrooms.

> The association also manages other unusual buildings (railway stations, former schools and a brewery), but unfortunately they have lost their original furnishings. Only the façades have been preserved.

LA TOUR DE CHIMAY (CHIMAY TOWER)

A 14th-century watchtower transformed into a self-catering flat

La tour de Chimay ❽
Mairie d'Aubenton
02500 Aubenton
Tel. 03 23 97 70 91
www.gites-de-France-aisne.
com/hebergement-13

ROOMS AND RATES
2 rooms, 5 people
180€–220€ per week,
depending on the season
Electric heating
Free wood
Washing machine, TV,
barbecue grill, towel and
sheet rental, freezer

Aubenton is a small village of the Thiérache region (northern Aisne) where Jean Mermoz, a famous French aviator, was born in 1901.

Located along the border between the kingdoms of France and Austria-Hungary, Aubenton was victim to the vengeance of the Count of Hainaut in 1340. After the massacre (2500 casualties), the clergy and the inhabitants united to build fortifications, since the wooden barricades hadn't succeeded in protecting the village.Descriptions mention the construction of a wall with 6 brick towers and 3 gates. Having long since become obsolete, the fortifications disappeared during the French Revolution. Only 2 towers survived: Chimay Tower and Daniel Tower. Highly modified in the 19th and 20th centuries, Chimay Tower was acquired by the town in 1979 and later transformed into a self-catering flat that can accommodate up to 5 people.

THE FORMER PRESBYTERY OF PARFONDEVAL

Spend the night in a house that serves as an entrance to one of France's most beautiful villages

THE FORMER PRESBYTERY OF PARFONDEVAL ❾
02630 Parfondeval
Contact: Demeures de Thiérache
Tel. 06 77 99 97 67
www.demeuresdethierache.com
demeuresdethierarche@initialite.com

ROOMS AND RATES
4 rooms
for 6 to 8 people
Weekend rate: 185€–275€, depending on the season
Week rate: 290€–485€, depending on the season

A typical village of the Thiérache region, Parfondeval is one of the most beautiful villages in France. During the reign of Louis XIII and Louis XIV, the villagers built a fortified church dedicated to Saint Medardus to defend the town from hordes of brigands. Around the church they built squat homes that served as ramparts, which explains why today the village seems to curl up into itself.

To get to the church, you pass through a gate that is an integral part of a house. It's this house, the village's former presbytery, that is available for rent. The home has all the modern amenities and is very well equipped.

LE NID DANS L'ARBRE

Use a Tyrolean traverse to reach this cabin in the trees

Le Nid dans l'arbre ⑩
5, impasse des Fermes
60350 Vieux Moulin
(mailing address:
directions to the cabins
will be given by phone)
Tel. 03 44 85 08 65
or 06 77 83 18 50
www.leniddanslarbre.com
contact@leniddanslarbre.fr

ROOMS AND RATES
8 treehouses,
7 of which are reached
by a Tyrolean traverse
(minimum age
requirement: 10 years)
3 duo houses (for 2 people):
130€–160€ per night
4 family houses
(for 2 to 5 people):
150€–200€ per night
1 family house
(for 4 to 8 people):
220€–360€ per night,
access by a staircase,
terrace (meets all
safety standards)
Open April to December,
generally (space heaters
provided on cool nights)
Breakfast included
Dinner basket (prepared by
a caterer): 20€ per person

Opened in May, 2008, "Le Nid dans L'arbre" (Nest in the Tree) is the result of a true friendship. Childhood friends Christophe and Agathe were reunited by chance, thanks to professional projects that put them on the same path. Christophe had opened a treetop adventure park, and Agathe was developing new businesses, and innovative projects in particular. Remembering the afternoons they had spent playing in the trees as young children, they decided to throw themselves into this cabin adventure.

The cabins of "Le Nid dans L'arbre" are located in the large oak trees of Pierrefonds' forest, in Christophe and Agathe's home region, the Oise. The cabins are 4m to 8m above the ground and are prettily decorated with secondhand and antique objects (in Zen, Breton, Gustavian or Scandinavian style). The only way to reach the cabins is by a Tyrolean traverse. Breakfast is served in a basket left at the bottom of the tree: you simply hoist it up when ready. The same system may be used for dinner – unless you bring your own picnic, of course.

To have the extraordinary opportunity to hear a stag's mating call (September to October), you should reserve early. It's a magical experience.

PARC CANOPÉE (CANOPY PARK)

Sleep in a hammock hung in the treetops

PARC CANOPÉE ⓫
Benoît Sautillet
Forêt de Chatel
5, rue Quillette
02290 Ambleny
Tel. 06 10 47 53 02
www.canopeeaventure.com
Ben.sautillet@orange.fr

ROOMS AND RATES
28 hammocks, including
one 2-person hammock
25€ per person and
35€ per person for
the "Plum'arbres"®
Minimum age requirement
for the hammocks
is 6 to 8 years old
Open Saturday evenings
in May and September,
and every night
in July and August

After its Accrobranche (tree-climbing) courses and bungee-jumping activities, which are offered both day and night, Parc Canopée (Canopy Park) decided to expand its business and offer overnight accommodation in hammocks or "Plum'arbres"® (hanging tents, see page 96) hung in pine trees at heights varying from 3m to 15m.

You reach the hammocks by ladder or, in a more athletic manner, by following a tree-climbing course. Then there's the difficult exercise of getting into the hammock, which, of course, quickly begins to rock.

Afterwards, you'll be given your pillow and sleeping-bag, and perhaps a book and flashlight. Finally, it's time for lights out and you're left to spend a night under the stars surrounded by the sounds of the forest and still attached to your harness in order to keep you from falling.

If the weather turns bad, don't worry. A supervisor will come quickly to lead everyone to shelter under a tent.

In the morning, breakfast is served in the forest.

LE CHÊNE PERCHÉ
To get back to nature, get high!

Le Chêne perché ⑫
Domaine de la Vénerie
08460 Signy l'Abbaye
Tel. 03 24 53 35 62
or 06 37 32 49 65
www.lecheneperche.com
infos@lecheneperche.com

Rooms and rates
4 tree-houses accommodating
2 to 8 people
85€–110€ per night
for 2 people,
depending on the tree-house
105€–115€ for 3 people
125€–135€ for 4 people
260€ for 8 people
Breakfast included,
served at the base of the tree
Bring your own sleeping-bag
Special prices for the treetop
activity courses (3 children's
courses with another for
children 6 years or younger
to open soon, 4 adult courses,
5 Tyrolean traverse courses)
Bike rental: mountain bikes,
hybrid bikes, tandem bikes,
and child bike trailers
Open April to November

It took 3 years for a team of passionate people to bring this park in the middle of Signy forest at the heart of the Ardennes region to life, with its treetop climbing courses and tree-houses offering overnight accommodation. The tree-houses are located either at the edge or at the heart of the forest, and they all offer a unique panorama of the valley and forest. You reach them by climbing a ladder and then taking a footbridge. Although specialized equipment isn't required, it would be best to avoid wearing high heels.

The Lisière and Sous-bois tree-houses (13m and 8m above ground respectively) can accommodate children 6 years or older. The Canopée tree-house, one of the highest in France, stands at a height of 16m and can accommodate children 14 years or older; one must climb 2 ladders and take a suspended footbridge to get to the top of the oaks.

Lastly, a final tree-house can accommodate up to 8 people, with no minimum age requirement, and is thus perfect for large families looking to gain some height (it has 3 levels ranging from 3m to 8m above ground).

None of the tree-houses has running water or electricity, but they do have eco-friendly toilets.

The park offers other activities, including mountain and tandem biking, pedagogical hikes for children, and various nature-related demonstrations to learn more about the forest.

HOSPITEL HÔTEL-DIEU

A hotel in a hospital overlooking Notre Dame Cathedral

HOSPITEL HÔTEL-DIEU ⑬
1, place du Parvis
Notre-Dame
Galerie B2, 6ᵉ étage
(6th floor)
75004 Paris
Tel. 01 44 32 01 00
www.hotel-hospitel.com
hospitelhoteldieu@
wanadoo.fr

ROOMS AND RATES
14 rooms
115€ per person,
126€ for 2 people
(reduced rates for patients
and their families)
Extra bed: 11€
Breakfast: 8€

Hôtel-Dieu Hospital is home to a little-known hotel that, contrary to what one might think, is not reserved solely for patients and their families, even if the possibility of coming across stretchers in the hallway is highly likely.

The 14 rooms are functional and even possess a flat-screen TV and wi-fi access.

The hotel is simple, clean, and, of course, very well located in the heart of Paris. If you're lucky enough to get a room on the east side, you'll even have a view of the towers of Notre Dame Cathedral.

Founded in 651 by Saint Landry, Bishop of Paris, Hôtel-Dieu is the oldest hospital in Paris and one of the first in France, and even in Western Europe.

Originally, it was a modest and simple refuge for the poor, built on the left bank of Île de la Cité, but it rapidly became a place to treat all the miseries of mankind. A refuge and symbol of human solidarity against physical and mental suffering, the hospital was destroyed by several fires and had to be raised from its ashes. The original structures, which had become too cramped and unfit, were replaced during the Second Empire by a new building located at the current site.

THE PARIS YACHT

Spend the night on a calm boat near Île de la Cité

THE PARIS YACHT ⓮
Bertrand Wilmart
11, quai Saint-Bernard
75005 Paris
Tel. 06 88 70 26 36
www.paris-yacht.com
contact@paris-yacht.com

ROOMS AND RATES
2 double cabins
for 2 to 4 people.
One has a lavatory,
and the other a shower,
sink and lavatory.
Note: reservations are
for the entire boat, regardless
of the number of passengers,
starting at 300€ a night
for 2 people, including
champagne and breakfast
(the manager leaves
everything you'll
need for your use)
Weekend rate: 500€
for 2 nights for 2 people (50€
for each additional guest)

ANOTHER UNUSUAL HOTEL
NEARBY

Docked at Port de la Tournelle, opposite Île Saint Louis and just steps from Notre Dame Cathedral, the Paris Yacht is a unique way to sleep on the Seine at water level, gently rocked by the soft lapping of the waves. The boat was built in 1933 by naval architect André Mauric, who also designed the first French vessel to participate in the America's Cup as well as competition sailboats, including the Pen Duick VI and the Kriter V. Based in Bastia where he monitored the Corsican coast under the codename "Golo", he participated in the search for Rommel's treasure before being transferred to the Gulf of Gascony.

In 1966, the Paris-Yacht, which had been refurbished to accommodate up to 65 people, returned to Paris and was used to transport passengers on the Burgundy Canal.

BATEAU JOHANA ⓯

The Bateau Johanna (Johanna Boat) is located at the heart of Paris, just steps away from the Orsay Museum, the Eiffel Tower, the Louvre, and the Tuileries Gardens. Purchased by the current owners in 1987, this former barge from Rotterdam (the Netherlands) originally transported concrete. During Paris' campaign to host the 2012 Olympic Games, the owners transformed the barge into a B&B with 2 charming little cabins. Part of the barge's interior is covered in varnished wood dating from 1936, the year of its construction.
- 2 nights minimum: 90€ for 1 person, 100€ for 2 people, 30€ for each additional guest in the second cabin
  Wi-fi access, satellite TV, parking
- Port de Solferino - Quai Anatole France - 75007 **Paris**
- Tel. 01 45 51 60 83
- www.bateau.johanna.free.fr • bateau.johanna@free.fr

HÔTEL AMOUR

For an hour, an afternoon or a night

HÔTEL AMOUR ⑯
8, rue de Navarin
75009 Paris
Tel. 01 48 78 31 80
www.hotelamourparis.fr
hotelamour@hotmail.fr

ROOMS AND RATES
24 rooms:
100€ for 1 person,
150€ to 250€ per
night for 2 people,
depending
on the size of the room
From 12pm to 3.30pm,
20% off the room rate
(call in the morning
to reserve)
Breakfast: 12€
(available until noon)
Restaurant and bar

Just a stone's throw away from rue des Martyrs, Hôtel Amour has become a neighbourhood hang-out.

Don't go looking for the hotel reception desk, the concierge or the porter, because there isn't one. There's no hotel entrance either, for that matter: you enter through the restaurant, where a staircase hidden behind a door leads to the rooms.

The rooms are all one-of-a-kind and blatantly sexy. The hotel's most significant characteristic, beside its name ("Love Hotel"), is the fact that the rooms can also be rented by the hour, which some of the neighbourhood's inhabitants apparently find quite useful...

If you're inviting friends, then you should reserve the Belvedere room, which has a private terrace and a large table that can seat up to 12 people. The vodka bar, conveniently placed in the room, can help set the ambience.

A bit cosier, the room designed by Alexandre de Bétak is entirely black with disco balls hanging from the ceiling. The bed rests on a raised platform opposite an antique bathtub and a frosted-glass mirror.

FLOBOAT AND BREAKFAST

A night on the water, just a stone's throw away from the Palace of Versailles

FLOBOAT AND BREAKFAST **17**
Péniche Rex
6, chemin du Halage
78560 Le Port Marly
Tel. 06 84 54 21 13 or 06 08
85 92 56 or 01 39 23 00 02
www.floboatandbreakfast.
com

ROOMS AND RATES
2 rooms
90€ for 1 person,
breakfast included,
100€ for 2 people
110€ for 2 adults and 1 child,
10€ for each additional child
TV, DVD player, High-speed
Internet connection

Built in 1930, the "Rex" barge spent many years transporting building materials, and gravel in particular. Florence fell in love with the barge and bought it, later transforming it to include two rooms.

Breakfast is served in the main room or on the terrace, weather permitting. It is also the perfect opportunity to meet Florence, who will eagerly share her happiness and experience of life on the water with you.

BATEAU ZEN (ZEN BOAT)

Spend a night on a former tugboat just 18km from Paris

BATEAU ZEN ⓲
Serge Lemonnier
Face au 96, quai de Seine
95530 La Frette sur Seine
Tel. 01 39 31 10 85
www.weekend-en-seine.eu
sergelemonnier@wanadoo.fr

ROOMS AND RATES
Self-catering rental
for 4 people
Weekend rate (Saturday
morning to Sunday night):
210€ for 2 people
Week rate: 490€ for 2 people
Not recommended for
children under 8
Open year round

The Bateau Zen (Zen Boat), a former tugboat built in 1926, could once pull up to a dozen barges at a time. Now that barges are motorized, there are fewer active tugboats. Serge was able to buy this one in 2008.

The boat, which is entirely made of wood, now has two 2-person rooms with Internet access, a television and a DVD player. It's a charming stopping-place just 18km from Paris.

GUEST COMMENTS

"We spent a wonderful weekend on the water. The barge is well located, welcoming and comfortable, and has retained its old-time charm. It was very relaxing and a true change of scenery. We hope to come back soon for another visit!"

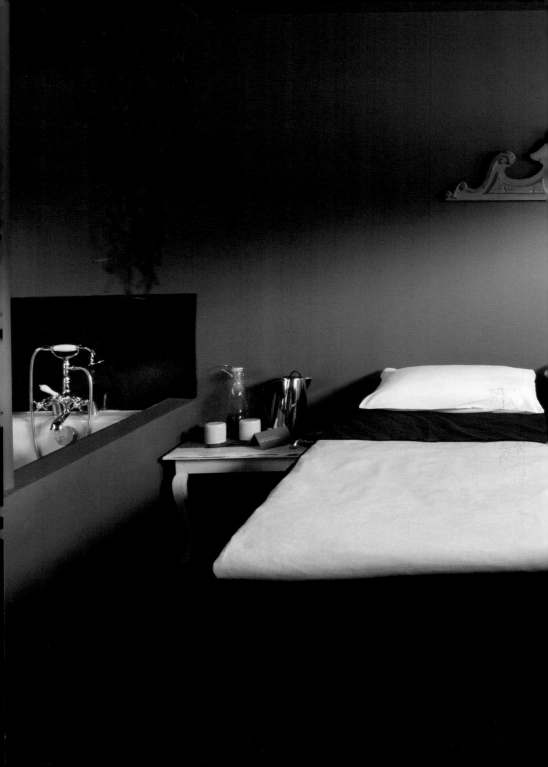

LE BOUDOIR DE SERENDIPITY

A barge in Asnières

LE BOUDOIR DE SERENDIPITY ⑲
Port Van Gogh
Quai Aulagnier
92600 Asnières-sur-Seine
Tel. 06 24 36 30 36
www.leboudoirdeserendipity.
com
contact@
leboudoirdeserendipity.com

ROOMS AND RATES
3 rooms
"Songe d'une nuit étoilée"
(Starry night dream),
unsinkable room:
115€ per night
"Des rêves par milliers"
(Dreams by the thousands):
165€ per night
"Comme un doux rêve"
(Like a sweet dream),
former captain's quarters:
165€ per night
Breakfast included
CD player, wi-fi access,
electric kettle and Nespresso
machine in each room,
and of course the little
surprises left by Marie

Docked at Van Gogh port in Asnières, Le Boudoir de Serendipity is a barge dating from 1930 that has welcomed guests since 2008.

Marie and Mickaël have designed 3 rooms decorated with antique and secondhand objects, family heirlooms and designer furniture.

In the summer, the barge's roof becomes a beautiful terrace. You can relax while gliding along the Seine, weather permitting.

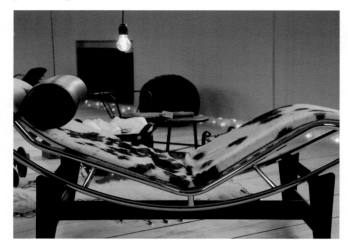

CHEZ BERTRAND

Spend the night in a refurbished 2CV car!

CHEZ BERTRAND [20]
93400 Saint Ouen
Tel. 06 63 19 19 87
www.chezbertrand.com
bonjourbertrand@gmail.com

ROOMS AND RATES
4 apartments
The Loft (5 people):
from 250€ for 2 nights
for 2 to 3 people,
to 580€ for 7 nights
The Studio (3 people):
from 230€ for 2 nights
to 500€ for 7 nights
The Duplex (6 people):
from 300€ for 2 nights
for 1 to 3 people,
to 770€ for 7 nights
for 5 to 8 people
"L'Appart" (5 people):
from 230€ for 2 nights
for 2 to 3 people,
to 570€ for 7 nights
for 4 to 5 people

Located just a few steps away from Saint Ouen's famous flea market, this former fireplace store was sold in 2006 to Bertrand, who kept the original façade but entirely renovated the interior into a 40m² loft, a duplex, a studio apartment, and his own apartment.

In the "garage"-style loft, an actual red 2CV convertible has been turned into an astonishing bed. Guests can even watch a movie (200 TV channels) on a large flat-screen TV "drive-in" style. A round bed lies behind the car.

Entirely covered in aluminum foil, the Studio is a veritable masterpiece: each sheet was crumpled, and then glued, before finally being protected with varnish. As for the shower, it was installed in a rain water tank.

In a nearby street at the heart of the flea market, the owner also refurbished "L'Appart" (The Flat): a very "love" red-and-white entryway, a rather girly pink bedroom (pink window film and pink walls), a living-room with green walls and a sofa bed, and a small orange kitchen with a disco ball. Children will love the Haribo boy whose body is filled with candy.

LES CABANES DE GRAVILLE
(THE GRAVILLE CABINS)

Treetop cabins in a chateau's private forest

LES CABANES DE GRAVILLE ㉑
Château de Graville
77670
Vernou-la-Celle-sur-Seine
Tel. 01 64 23 08 87
or 06 21 77 16 64
www.lacabanedegraville.com
dianedesdigueres@
wanadoo.fr

ROOMS AND RATES
4 cabins
120€ per night
for 2 people, breakfast
included

After having created adventure trails through the 990-acre protected private forest on his property a few years ago, the owner of the chateau of Graville, on the suggestion of one of his friends, had 4 tree-house cabins built in ancient oak trees (one of which is more than 300 years old) at heights ranging from 6m to 9m above ground.

Capable of accommodating two people each, the cabins are accessible by a simple stepladder, or, for the more athletic, by rope ladders and harnesses.

The cabins have neither electricity nor running water. Guests are advised to bring a sleeping-bag and a fully charged mobile phone. However, there are showers in the chateau (and dry toilets in the cabins).

On the property, guests can enjoy horse riding or a ride in a hot-air balloon.

MUSEUMOTEL L'UTOPIE

A one-of-a-kind place

MUSEUMOTEL L'UTOPIE 🞁
Île Haüsermann
88110 Raon l'Étape
Tel. 03 29 50 48 81
www.museumotel.com
museumotel@orange.fr

ROOMS AND RATES
9 bubble-bungalows
for 1 to 5 people
55€ to 100€
for 1 person
85€ to 100€ for 2 people
Additional person: 10€
Breakfast: 7€
Various packages
including champagne
and breakfast are available

The utopian and visionary architect Pascal Haüsermann built this extravagant, even outrageous, place in 1967 and 1968 on a site surrounded by two branches of a river. The first motel, which operated from 1968 to 1998, remained closed for 4 years before being bought and reopened in 2007. The original "pop" theme was kept, but all modern amenities were added.

The site is now a motel, an eco-museum and a place for artistic expression. You can spend the night, have a drink at the Utopia café (serving Breizh cola, poppy -or violet-flavoured drinks, and more), visit an art exhibit, attend a concert, or simply stroll through the garden among the contemporary sculptures.

The bubble-bungalows, which respect all the styles from the 1950s to the 1970s and are furnished with period designer furniture (Charles Eames, Verner Panton), are each decorated in a unique and personalized manner. They each have a shower, sink and toilet.

Among the different bungalows, there's the "Love Bubble" with its heart-shaped double bed, and the orange "69" bubble whose psychedelic plastic décor will delight fans of the 1970s.

LA FERME AVENTURE (ADVENTURE FARM)

Spend the night in a plane, a glass pyramid, or on a bed of straw in a hayloft

La Ferme aventure ㉓
15, Côte de Hardémont
88240 La Chapelle aux Bois
Tel. 03 29 30 11 79
www.nuitsinsolites.com
lfaventure@free.fr

ROOMS AND RATES
Tree-house
(2 to 5 people):
90€ per night
Caravelle (2 to 6 people):
100€ per night (25€ heating
charge November to March)
Pyramid:
90€ per night
Yurt (2 to 5 people):
90€ per night
4 tipis,
2 small tipis for children
(2 to 10 people):
62€ per night
4 hayloft rooms
(2 to 10 people):
62€ per night
16€ per additional guest
Open year round.
Closed from Christmas
to New Year's Day
Tipis and haylofts
closed in winter

On the property of Denis Duchêne and his son Benoît, the options for spending an unusual night are quite numerous: you can sleep in a tree-house, a yurt or a tipi, or, if you're looking for something even more original, you can sleep in a glass pyramid or a real Caravelle airplane. Construction of the Caravelle, the flagship of French aviation, began in 1955; 282 were built. Baptized Ohrid (after a lake on the border of Albany and Macedonia), the Caravelle 233 that Denis bought had 20,000 registered flight hours and had taken its last flight in the colours of the Corsair airline before being dismantled and transported to the Vosges mountains. Today, it has been transformed into a loft, with a living-room, bedrooms, barbecue grill, and a 3000m² enclosed lawn.

For those who dream of sleeping under the stars, but in warmth and sheltered from wild animals, the glass pyramid offers a truly unique experience. There are no curtains on the windows, but the pyramid is far enough away from the other buildings to ensure your privacy.

A final experience is to spend the night in a hayloft on a bed of straw.

BRANCHES ET MONTAGNES
(BRANCHES AND MOUNTAINS)

A night in the trees

BRANCHES ET MONTAGNES ㉔
Lac Blanc 1200
68370 Orbey
Tel. 03 89 71 29 18
www.branches-et-montagnes.
com
info@branches-et-montagnes.
com

ROOMS AND RATES
50€ per person,
breakfast included
By reservation
from May to September,
depending on the weather
Minimum of 4 people
Children must be
at least 10 years old

Generally, sunset marks the end of a hike through the forest. In the company of the guides of Branches et Montagnes (Branches and Mountains), however, it means the adventure is just starting. Specialized in outdoor activities, this company invites you to spend a night in the trees.

The adventure thus begins with an introduction to tree climbing. Trainers are present to supervise the entire activity (1 trainer for every 4 participants), which is not always the case in a typical Accrobranche (tree-climbing) park. No ropes, footbridges, or zip-cords have been installed in the trees: you are secured from the top with harnesses and you climb different trees, from the easiest with branches arranged like stairs, to the more complicated, which require a bit more agility.

Although the original hammocks were quite poetic, they were, in fact, rather uncomfortable. Now, guests sleep at a height of 4m to 8m above ground on a platform equipped with a mattress and a canvas tent.

The roof can even be opened to let you admire the leaves and the canopy of heaven from your bed. Before going to sleep, guests put on a harness in order to eliminate any chance of falling.

The evening meal is a picnic that guests bring, along with their own sleeping-bag and flashlight.

For guests who get up often during the night, the solution is simple for men. For women, there are dry toilets nearby.

LE CARRÉ ROUGE (RED SQUARE)

Sleep in a red cube with no running water or electricity

LE CARRÉ ROUGE **25**
Route de Santenoge
52160 Villars-Santenoge
Haute-Marne, southern part
of the Langres plateau
Tel. 06 62 03 98 38
www.leconsortium.
com/carrerg
jf.guenin@free.fr

ROOMS AND RATES
130€ for the weekend
plus 30€ per extra day
(e.g. 190€ for 4 days)
1 to 6 people (maximum
occupancy: 6 people)
Sheets, comforters,
blankets, pillows, towels,
dishes, wood for cooking
and heating, as well as
gas lamps are provided

DIRECTIONS
From Paris by car,
on the A5, take exit
Langres-sud. On the A6,
take the exit Auxerre-sud,
then Chablis, Tonnere,
Châtillon-sur-Seine, and
Recey-sur-Ource. At Recey,
take the road to Langres.
At Villars-Santenoge,
follow the road to Chaugey.
At the old wash house,
turn right on the road
to the Chalmandrier Farm
(ferme Chalmandrier).

A masterpiece of contemporary art by Gloria Friedmann, the Carré Rouge (Red Square) is a cube with a south-facing side painted red and a north-facing side made entirely of glass. Lost in the middle of the French countryside on the Langres plateau, the site is superb – the perfect place for a unique, romantic getaway or a family vacation.

The cube has two levels: the lower level holds the kitchen and dining space, while the upper level houses three double beds.

Without running water or electricity, staying in the cube is a return to a more primitive state that will delight children. Rainwater is collected by a water pump, and potable water is available at the village fountains, just a short walk away (700m). For lighting, oil lamps and candles are available, as is the woodstove (no need to cut the wood, it's graciously provided!) which serves for both cooking and heating, thanks to a central pipe that diffuses the heat throughout the cube.

Jean-François Guénin, the manager, runs an equestrian centre just a short distance from the cube. Guests can thus go horse riding through the surrounding forests and hills.

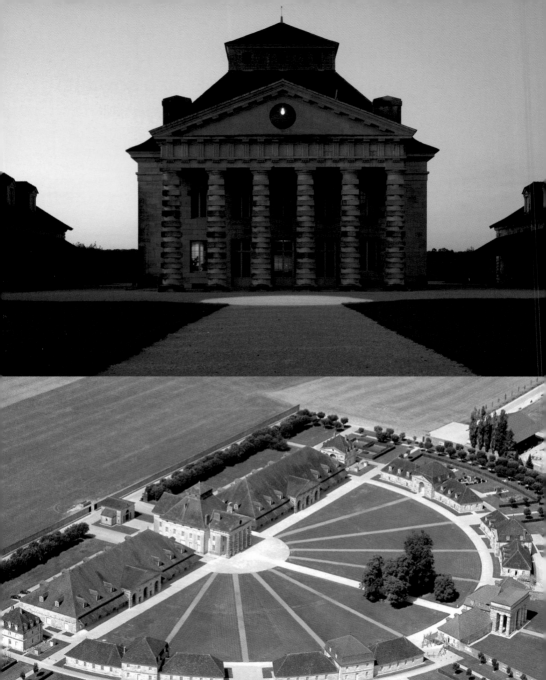

SALINE ROYALE (ROYAL SALTWORKS)

Spend the night in an exceptional historic monument

SALINE ROYALE ❷⓪
25610 Arc et Senans
Tel. 03 81 54 45 00
www.salineroyale.com
colloques@salineroyale.com

ROOMS AND RATES
12 rooms: 70€ to 90€
for 2 people,
depending on the room
and the season,
includes entrance
to the Saltworks
(site and museums)
Buffet breakfast: 10€

Built on the order of Louis XV, the Saline Royale (Royal Saltworks) of Arc and Senans is the masterpiece of Claude-Nicolas Ledoux. Classified as a world heritage site by UNESCO, this monument was built from 1775 to 1779 to recuperate salt from low-content salt water.

After the end of this industrial activity in 1895, the 11 buildings were saved from destruction many times, and, now restored, they are the site of cultural activities, seminars, colloquiums and artist studios. Although the Saltworks is not actually a hotel, it is possible to stay there.

Twelve comfortable rooms restored by architect Wilmotte (others will soon be available) welcome guests in a sharp, clean style. The architect even designed the furniture, which was then manufactured by the Saline Royale engineering department with wood from the nearby Chaux forest, the second largest natural forest in France. In fact, it was partly due to this forest that the Saltworks was built here. In addition to the northern winds which, by simple evaporation, gave the brine a much higher salt concentration before being heated, the abundant quantity of wood was an essential element in the production of salt: it was used to heat, evaporate and transform the brine.

It is when the tourists have left that guests truly realize what a privilege it is to spend the night at this historic site.

The diversity of the Saltworks' activities means guests can meet conference participants in suits, performers rehearsing (Jane Birkin was recently sighted here) or gardeners working for the Garden Festival held every year from June to October.

It was through the œil-de-boeuf window in the central building, which housed the director's office, that the latter kept watch over the Saltworks.

LES GRENIERS DU MEIX-LAGOR
(MEIX-LAGOR LOFTS)

Lofts installed in an old shed

LES GRENIERS DU MEIX-LAGOR ㉗
25500 Montlebon
Tel. 03 81 67 26 03
www.meix-lagor.fr
info@meix-lagor.fr

ROOMS AND RATES
A self-catering lodge
with 6 rooms,
capable of accommodating
15 to 18 people
Weekend rate
(Friday night to
Monday morning):
1700€
Week rate
(Saturday to Saturday):
2200€ to 3200€
depending on the season
Open year round

Located 1100m above sea level a few kilometres from the Swiss border, the Greniers du Meix-Lagor (Meix-Lagor Lofts) are the result of a hard-working family that arrived here with their sheep in 1978, and who opened a small café that quickly became a restaurant. Then, in 2004, they opened their self-catering lofts to welcome passing guests.

The haylofts were found at various places throughout the region and were then swept out, cleaned, dismantled and reinstalled in an old shed, which was also renovated, to create a sort of interior village. Guests thus find themselves in astonishing little house-rooms surrounding a village-type square that serves as a common space for all the guests.

The self-catering lodge is very comfortable. In addition to a television and DVD player, there is a jacuzzi (in a former copper cauldron used to make Comté cheese), sauna, hammam, solarium, and a natural pool.

The region offers numerous outdoor activities, and the lofts are open year-round. In the summer, you can go hiking, spelunking, canyoning or mountain biking; in the winter, you can try your hand at cross-country skiing (the trails pass at the foot of the lofts), dog-sledding or ice-skating on Switzerland's Taillères Lake, before relaxing in one of Yverdon's thermal baths.

On the evening of your arrival, a traditional raclette dinner (melted cheese served over boiled potatoes and cured meats) will be served. You may enjoy other meals in the lodge or in the 200-year-old inn with its stone walls and wood fireplace.

A truly convivial place where stress disappears as if by magic.

DOMAINE DE SYAM

One of the highest cabins in France

DOMAINE DE SYAM 🕸
240, rue Rengourd
39300 Syam
Tel. 03 84 44 72 40
or 03 84 51 64 87
www.domaine-de-syam.com
Annie.gay@wanadoo.fr

ROOMS AND RATES
6 tree cabins,
including the highest
cabin in France
with modern amenities
150€ per night for 2 people,
2-night minimum rental
700€ per week
in June and September
805€ per week
in July and August
50€ per day for each
additional person
12 years or older
25€ for additional guests
younger than 12
20% off for stays
of 3 nights or more
Bring your own sheets
or sleeping-bags
Open May to September
The Pigeon Roost:
60m² self-catering cottage
for 2 to 3 people:
590€ per week

The château of Syam's current owners, who are enthusiasts of historic monuments and their restoration, bought this property in a ruinous state in 1990. The edifice, an 18th-century château that was transformed into a large Neo-Classical manor in 1817 by the founders of the forge-master dynasty, the Jobez family, is listed on France's *inventaire supplémentaire des monuments historiques* (supplementary inventory of historic monuments). The forge nearby was in operation until 2009.

After completing major work on the château, the owners decided to have two, and then four, cabins built in the trees at heights varying from 6m to 18m above ground. The larger ones can accommodate 2 to 4 people, and some even have a terrace or balcony. Set in the trees or on poles (we strongly suggest the former option as it is much more romantic), the cabins were built by a company specialized in cabin building. A simple stairway leads to each cabin.

The highest cabin, the Fauconnière (Falcon's Roost), stands at 18m above ground and is the highest cabin in France to include a shower and kitchen.

Nearby, you'll find a stunning Neo-Palladian villa that Emmanuel Jobez, one of the heirs of the dynasty, had built at the other end of the English garden in 1825; the famous villa La Rotonda in Vincenza, Italy, served as a model. Unfortunately, he died in 1828 without seeing the villa's completion in 1840.

> For more information, we recommend the book written by the owner, Annie Gay, Les Jobez: Maîtres des Forges Jurassions au XIXᵉ siècle (currently only available in French).

> The former pigeon roost has also been turned into a self-catering cottage.

GUEST COMMENTS
"It's both calm and comfortable. We didn't expect to feel so at home. We tried to find some drawbacks, but there aren't any."

CABANES SUR PILOTIS

A cabin in the middle of a pond

CABANES SUR PILOTIS ㉙
Marolle
71190 Saint-Didier-
sur-Arroux
Tel. 03 85 82 31 14
www.cabanes-sur-pilotis.com
cabanessurpilotis@gmail.com

ROOMS AND RATES
1 cabin
120€ per night
for 2 people,
breakfast included
Picnic meals available for 20€
Open year round

The Cabane sur Pilotis (Cabin on Piles) of Saint-Didier-sur-Arroux isn't a simple lakeside cabin: it stands in the middle of a pond.

Accessible only by boat, the cabin is a little Robinson Crusoe-inspired dream that invites guests to experience the feeling of being cut off from the world.

This stockbreeding family's idea was born when a heavy storm toppled several oak trees, which they couldn't sell due to the oversaturated market. Built entirely by the 6 members of the family, the cabin is designed to accommodate a couple, and possibly a small child.

A small warning: access to the mezzanine, where the double bed is, is provided by a rather steep wooden ladder.

In the morning, breakfast is delivered on the bank of the pond, so you have to retrieve it by boat before enjoying it on the terrace while surrounded by silence, sheep-filled meadows, squirrels, and the sound of the carp in the water. You'll feel like you are experiencing the first morning on earth.

Beyond the bank, in a small clearing, a small outdoor parlour of wood furniture is equipped with a barbecue grill. The owner also offers picnic meals made from regional and home-made products: cured ham, goat cheese, fromage frais (a creamy soft cheese), and garden-fresh fruit and vegetables.

Guests can also go fishing and swimming in the pond.

The town of Autun is just a few kilometres away.

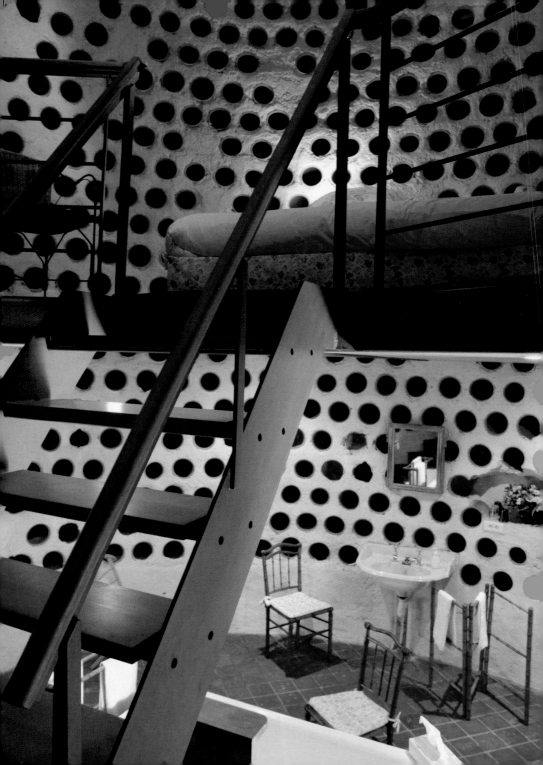

LA FERTÉ ABBEY DOVECOTE

A beautiful dovecote at the heart of an abbey

LA FERTÉ ABBEY DOVECOTE ③⓪
Mr. and Mrs.
Jacques Thénard
La Ferté sur Grosne
71240 Saint Ambreuil
Tel. 03 85 44 17 96
www.abbayeferte.com
abbayedelaferte@aol.com

ROOMS AND RATES
Dovecote: 2-room suite
with a bathroom:
75€ for 2 people
Open May to September
Gatehouse: 95€ for 2 people
Open Easter to mid-October

La Ferté Abbey is a classified historic monument from the 18th century. It was the first abbey to be founded by Saint Bernard in 1113, and was one of the largest Cistercian abbeys in France.

Although the church disappeared after the French Revolution, the ancestors of the current owners, who bought the site, preserved the superb 70m-long abbey residence. The monks' magnificent former refectory has been converted into a reception hall.

The abbey also possesses a rather exceptional dovecote: it still has the cells where the birds nested, which is rare nowadays. A beautiful bathroom has been installed, and, on the mezzanine level, you'll find a bedroom with a double bed.

The gatehouse at the entrance to the abbey was the home of the monk gatekeeper, who was in charge of monitoring visitors. It has also been charmingly restored and turned into guest-rooms.

The English-style park that surrounds the abbey invites guests to take a pleasurable stroll.

> It is also possible to visit the entire domain in the company of the owner.

WEST

DOVECOTE SELF-CATERING COTTAGE

Sleep in a true historic dovecote

DOVECOTE SELF-CATERING COTTAGE 🛈
Yves and Michèle Bouquet
126, Bout de la ville
76550 Offranville
Tel. 02 35 85 40 50
www.gite-colombier.fr
yves.michele@gite-colombier.fr

ROOMS AND RATES
1 cottage
(2 rooms accommodating
up to 6 people)
Weekend: 420€ to 480€
(except July and August)
Week: 640€ to 920€,
depending on the season

Since 2006, the 16th-century dovecote of Offranville has served as a charming and comfortable self-catering cottage. It is probably one of the few self-catering dovecotes in France that still has its original structure. Here, the ground floor has been transformed into a parlour with a fireplace, dining-room and kitchenette, while the upper floors hold 2 beautiful bedrooms and a bathroom. The dovecote stands in the middle of a farm just a few kilometres from the cliffs of the Alabaster Coast and the Pays de Caux region.

LE JARDIN DE LA LICORNE
(THE UNICORN'S GARDEN)

Spend the night in a 1950s British bus

LE JARDIN DE LA LICORNE ㉜
14130 Les Authieux-
sur-Calonne
Tel. 06 87 06 69 01
www.gite-roulotte-
deauville-honfleur.com
jardin-de-la-licorne@
wanadoo.fr

ROOMS AND RATES
1 British bus for 4/5 people
1 caravan for 4 people
3 caravans for 2/3 people
Rented as self-catering
cottages (no breakfast)
Sheets and towels
are provided
Bus: 100€ per night
or 190€ for the weekend
Caravans: 90€ per night
or 160€ for the weekend
Open mid-February
to mid-November (heated)

Antoine has installed some very charming caravans in his garden (the oldest is 110 years old). With his circus caravans or movie caravan dating from the 70s, he was one of the pioneers of this trend in France (see the many other caravans in France offering overnight accommodation), but, in a more original manner, he has also outfitted an astonishing British bus.

The bus, which is rather impressively carpeted in a red Scottish motif, is equipped with 2 double beds, a vintage bar with original seats, a shower and a kitchenette.

The site is stunning and pleasant, just 7km from Pont-l'Évêque and 18km from Deauville.

The property also includes a sculpture studio that is open on Saturday afternoon.

DOMAINE DE LA COUR AU GRIP

"Spending the night in a barrel? Simply intoxicating."

DOMAINE DE LA COUR AU GRIP 🤍
Mr and Mrs Esnard
14340 Repentigny
Tel. 02 31 63 85 85
or 06 72 78 53 72
http://lacouraugrip.
blog.capital.fr
paulette.esnard@wanadoo.fr

ROOMS AND RATES
90€ for 2 people,
gourmet breakfast included
Reduced rates for stays
of 3 nights or more
Table d'hôte dinner:
25€, includes cocktail,
appetizer and a half-bottle
of cider (regional specialties
made with cider or
international cuisine)

At the heart of Normandy's Cider Route, just a few kilometres from Beuvron-en-Auge (which is listed among the most beautiful villages in France), lies the 19th-century cider-making property of Paulette and Patrick, with its beautiful half-timbered house that is so typical of the region.

The estate possesses several buildings reminiscent of its origins: cheese dairy, sheep barn, stable, cider houses, distillery, and, most importantly, a cider press, from which Paulette and Patrick salvaged cider barrels. Whereas some of them served to decorate the kitchen or were turned into furniture, Patrick took one and turned it into a cabin for his children. Then they added a table and chairs, and it became the place where they enjoyed a cocktail or dinner. And then one day they wondered why they couldn't sleep there ... And then one day they wondered why they couldn't sleep there, too, which is why guests can now spend the night in a 10,000-litre barrel!

Don't miss Paulette's table d'hôte dinners and culinary classes (she once taught in a catering school).

CHÂTEAU DE CANON

Europe's highest tree-house

CHÂTEAU DE CANON ❸❹
14720 Mézidon-Canon
Tel. 02 50 67 10 74
or 06 15 41 85 90
www.coupdecanon.fr
coupdecanon@gmail.com

ROOMS AND RATES
3 tree-houses
120€ to 180€ per night,
breakfast and complimentary
cocktail included
Dinner: 25€
Open year round
Heating provided in winter

Three spectacular tree-houses have been built in the park of the beautiful 18th-century château of Canon.

The Laizon tree-house stands 10m above ground, and the Cascade tree-house, at 16m above ground, was the highest in France at the time of its construction, but it's the château of Canon's third tree-house that is the highest in Europe, at 22m above ground.

It is smaller than the others, but it offers the same charm and comfort, which means it's of very high quality.

In the morning, guests hoist their own breakfast up to the tree-house: hot drinks, croissants, chocolate croissants, and organic apple juice.

It is also possible to order an evening meal, prepared by a caterer, that you can enjoy in your tree-house in the romantic glow of candlelight or an oil lamp.

PERCHÉ DANS LE PERCHE

Perched in the Le Perche park, as its name indicates

PERCHÉ DANS LE PERCHE **35**
Claire Stickland
La Renardière
61130 Bellou-le-Trichard
Tel. 02 33 25 57 96
www.perchedansleperche.com
perchedansleperche@
gmail.com

ROOMS AND RATES
150€ for 2 people,
breakfast included
20€ for each additional
person
2-night minimum
on weekends,
bank holidays
and school holidays
(250€ for 2 nights
for 2 people)
795€ for 2 people
for 1 week (7 nights),
breakfast included

After having lived in the Perche region for several years, Claire and Ivan decided to have a tree-house built in and around two beautiful chestnut trees. The tree-house can accommodate up to 5 people comfortably: small kitchen, corner dining area with bench seats, deckchairs, outdoor table and chairs, games and books for the kids, and more.

In the tree-house, you'll find binoculars and guidebooks, and the owners offer special astronomy-themed weekend getaways in relation to regional events, and notably those organized by the Le Perche Nature Park.

Every morning, Claire brings her guests a breakfast basket filled with home-made goods and regional (often organic) products.

DOMAINE DU BOIS LANDRY

Tree-houses at the heart of a private forest

DOMAINE DU BOIS LANDRY ㊱
Lieu-dit La Graiserie
28240 Champrond-en-Gâtine
Tel. 02 37 49 80 01
www.boislandry.com
contact@forestis.fr

ROOMS AND RATES
14 tree-houses with a
capacity of 2 to 6 people
115€ for 2 people,
breakfast included
31€ to 41€ for each
additional person
Tree-house dinner:
25€ per person
Optional extras:
cocktails, flower bouquets,
birthday cakes
Open from mid-February
to mid-November
(Note: the tree-houses
are not heated)

The Landry Woods estate is located in a 3000-acre private forest on the edge of the Le Perche Nature Park. Fourteen tree-houses, each with an open outlook, are dispersed over 75 acres. Some are along the bank of a pond, while others are in the heart of the forest. Standing at heights varying from 4m to 13m above ground, they are all reached by a simple staircase, ladder or a short tree-climbing course.

Each tree-house is different, and some are connected so they can accommodate up to 6 people, including young children.

Inside, you'll find no electricity or running water, but there are dry toilets, and candles and linens are furnished.

Breakfast is served in a basket that you hoist up to your tree-house.

The hunting lodge has been transformed into an office, conference rooms and bathrooms/showers.

FORT DU CAP LÉVI

Spend the night in an old Napoleonic fort

FORT DU CAP LÉVI ⊕
Isabelle Fremont
50840 Fermanville
Tel. 02 33 23 68 68
http://lefortducaplevi.
pagesperso-orange.fr/

ROOMS AND RATES
5 rooms,
including a family-size
room for up to 5 people
65€ for 2 people,
or 70€ for a room
with an ocean view
90€ for 3 people
25€ for each
additional person
Breakfast included
Closed in December
and January

The Cap Lévi fort was one of 12 batteries built at the beginning of the 19th century under Napoleon's orders to defend the Cotentin Peninsula from British attacks.

After having lost its military functions in the early 20th century, the fort resumed its service during World War I, and was then occupied during World War II. It ultimately became private property in 1953. It is now possible to spend the night in this historic ocean-front site.

Located between the famous Port Racine (the smallest port in France) and the large Gatteville Lighthouse, the Cap Lévi fort stands at the heart of a vast natural park protected by the Conservatoire du Littoral (Coastal Protection Agency). From the winter-garden overlooking the sea, where breakfast is served, you can see the harbour of Cherbourg in the distance.

THE AQUARIUM OF SAINT-MALO

A night among the sharks

THE AQUARIUM OF SAINT-MALO ❸❽
Avenue du Général Patton
35402 Saint-Malo
Information and reservations
Tel. 02 99 21 19 07
www.aquarium-st-malo.com
contact@aquarium-st-malo.com

ROOMS AND RATES
300€ (for 3 people)
100€ for each
additional person
(80€ for children
ages 6 to 14)
Group rates
(5 person minimum):
Adult: 90€, child: 70€
Optional "extra" package:
150€, includes shark feeding
by a diver, champagne
and an assortment of
regional cakes and cookies
10 people maximum
per night
Mattresses are provided.
Bring a sleeping-bag.
Please arrive at 8pm, after
having already had dinner

Everyone knows of the Great Aquarium of Saint-Malo, but few know that you can spend the night there. No diving suit or oxygen tank is necessary – you'll just need a sleeping-bag. Indeed, protected by the glass, evening visitors can spend an extraordinary night up-close with marine animals.

The evening begins aboard the Nautibus (inspired by the Nautilus of Jules Verne's famous novel *20,000 Leagues Under the Sea*), a veritable submarine that holds up to 5 people and that leads visitors on a voyage to the centre of the ocean. Then, after an all-inclusive visit of the aquarium, including a "backstage tour" of the quarantine and filtration rooms, it's time for bed (10pm).

The spectacular "Shark ring", a 360° room where 8 sharks swim about (the largest is 3m long) in the company of 4 turtles and a giant grouper, is where the guests sleep. In the morning, you can watch the sharks gulp down their morning meal before enjoying your own breakfast, still surrounded by tropical fish.

An absolutely singular experience.

THE PETIT MOULIN'S TREE HOUSES

Near an old mill

THE PETIT MOULIN'S TREE HOUSES ❸❾
Le Petit Moulin du Rouvre
35720 Saint-Pierre de Plesguen
Tel. 02 99 73 85 84
www.aumoulindurouvre.com
info@aumoulindurouvre.com

ROOMS AND RATES
4 cabins,
including 3 tree-houses
108€ for 2 people,
breakfast included
20€ for each additional person
Meal (served in the cabin)
with starter, main course
and dessert: 21€
7-acre park, 2.5-acre pond
Open year round (space heater
provided if necessary)

In 2006, Régis had 4 cabins built, one on an island and 3 as tree-houses, on the grounds of an old mill built in 1628.

Easily accessible by stairs or a small bridge, the tree-houses have neither electricity nor running water (they do have dry toilets), yet they are quite comfortable.

The property bears the name of the Rouvre oak trees that line the nearby fields. After being destroyed during World War I and then by a fire, the mill was sold to Régis' grandfather in 1968.

ANOTHER UNUSUAL HOTEL **NEARBY**

LE MANOIR DE L'ALLEU ❹⓪

Le Manoir de l'Alleu is a 17th-century manor surrounded by a tree-filled 7-acre park. In addition to traditional rooms, it also has 2 tree-houses designed around the Brocéliande Forest theme. On the terrace, a table and 2 chairs invite guests to fully enjoy their natural surroundings. The tree-houses have neither electricity nor running water (space heaters are provided in winter).

- 2 tree-houses: 110€ per night for 2 people (2 adults or 1 adult and 1 child aged 13 or over), breakfast included
- Table d'hôte dinner, by reservation (20€ per person, cocktail, wine and coffee included) or possibility to have a dinner-basket served in the tree-house, includes a hot dish (home-made with organic products), dessert and drink (30€ for 2 people)
- Laure and Bruno Goude - 35630 **La Chapelle Chaussée**
- Tel. 02 99 60 21 74 or 06 83 86 62 85
- goudefamilly@wanadoo.fr • www.manoir-de-lalleu.com

THE CHÂTEAU DU VAL D'ARGUENON'S TREE HOUSES

Tree-houses in exceptional trees

THE CHÂTEAU DU VAL D'ARGUENON'S TREE HOUSES ❹
Notre-Dame de Guildo
22380 Saint-Cast-le-Guildo
Tel. 02 96 41 07 03
www.chateauduval.com
chateau@chateauduval.com

ROOMS AND RATES
3 two-person tree-houses
115€ per night,
breakfast included
(delivered at 9am at
the base of the tree)
Bring a fully charged
mobile phone
Tennis court

If magical and enchanted places exist, then the Château du Val d'Arguenon is one of them. Owned by the same family for centuries (the château was sold once, but was bought back a few years later by a relative), it is now home to a large, welcoming family whose members each participate in welcoming guests or taking care of the magnificent 50-acre grounds that are home to a large number of palm trees.

The property occupies a unique location. A narrow drive at the bend of the road from Notre-Dame de Guildo to Saint-Cast-le-Guildo leads to the château. Park your car behind the château, then walk around to admire the view of the sound and small beaches waiting to welcome you. The ever-changing light is a magnificent spectacle that you can continue to admire from your treetop bedroom or tree-house terrace.

The property's beautiful trees are home to 3 tree-houses. The distance between them leaves guests with the feeling that they are alone in the world, which lets them fully appreciate this little corner of heaven.

PLUM'ARBRES®

A tent hanging from a tree

PLUM'ARBRES® ㊷
Á un fil
Tremargat (22)
Belle Ile (56)
Other sites welcome
Plum'Arbres® tents each year
Tel. 06 85 63 63 67
or 02 96 36 58 87
www.a-un-fil.com
info@a-un-fil.com

ROOMS AND RATES
Nights at heights
of 2m or less:
40€ per night for 2 people
Nights at heights
of more than 2m:
80€ per night for 2 people
Tent capacity: 2 adults
and 1 or 2 young children
(reduced rates for children)
Breakfast: 4.50€
(in partnership with
local businesses)
Meal: 12€ to 18€
Bring your own
sleeping-bag,
flashlight and fully
charged mobile phone.
Stays are cancelled
during thunderstorms
or strong winds.
Open May to September

Specialized in hanging furniture, the "Á un fil" company has recently begun offering a new way to sleep in the trees. Since tree-houses have become a classic among the "unusual" ways to spend the night, they had to find something more inventive and extreme. That is how hanging camping was born.

The concept is simple – guests spend the night in a tent hung from a tree.

With a floor made out of catamaran netting and customized mattresses, some guests have claimed that they slept better here than in their own home!

The highest tents hang about 12m above ground. The less brave can choose to sleep at a much lower height, which makes it easier to get in and out of the tent.

GUEST COMMENTS
"It has a pleasant rocking motion, and it's soft, warm and comfortable."

SELF-CATERING COTTAGES ON MILLIAU ISLAND

Self-catering cottages on a (nearly) deserted island

SELF-CATERING COTTAGES ON MILLIAU ISLAND ❸
Gîtes de l'île Milliau
Contact: Tourist office
Place Crec'h Heéy
22560 Trebeurden
Tel. 02 96 23 51 64
www.trebeurden.fr
tourisme@trebeurden.fr

ROOMS AND RATES
3 cottages
Bihit cottage: 3 people:
65€ per night
Toëno cottage: 5 people:
95€ per night
Castel cottage: 7 people:
125€ per night
or 17€ per person
Open from 1 April
to 30 September

Milliau Island is a 57-acre island near the port of Trebeurden in the Côtes d'Armor region. You can spend the night there, which means that once the last visitors have left, you'll be all alone, with the 70 animal species that have made their home on the island as your only company.

Although the island was first inhabited in the Neolithic period (6000 BC), the main buildings of the farm that still stands today were built in the 18th century. At the beginning of the 20th century, the Count of Carcaradec ceded the island to Mademoiselle de Jourdan, Aristide Briand's mistress. After her lover's death, the island fell into disuse. Fully abandoned after World War II, the island became the property of the French Coastal Protection Agency (Conservatoire du littoral) in 1984. The agency renovated the old farm built in pink granite, making it fully independent: a stream supplies the house with fresh water and solar panels were installed to produce electricity.

Milliau Island can be reached by boat, or by walking a 100m-long path that is revealed during low tide (tidal coefficient of 52 or more).

LOUËT ISLAND

Treat yourself to an island, without spending a fortune

LOUËT ISLAND 44
29660 Carantec
Tel. 02 98 67 00 43
www.carantec-tourisme.com
info@carantec-tourisme.com

ROOMS AND RATES
Capacity: 10 people
(8 in the house,
and 2 in the labourer's
workhouse)
184€ for 1 day and 1 night
(or 18.40€ per person
for a group of 10)
246€ for 2 days and 2 nights
(maximum length of stay)
Open from the end
of May to the beginning
of November (no heating)
Transport to island available
on demand by contacting
Carantec Nautisme
(Carantec Water Sports)
Bring a mobile phone,
sheets, pillowcases
and sleeping-bags

Louët Island is located in Morlaix Bay, 350m off the coast of Carantec. On a breathtaking site opposite the Château du Taureau, a rocky peak is home to the island's famous white lighthouse, which is featured in numerous books about Brittany. The lighthouse was inaugurated on 31 December 1860, and later automated in the 1960s. In 1998, the Lighthouse and Beacon administration placed it in under the management of the village of Carantec, which decided to open it up to the public.

Note that guests sleep in the lighthouse-keeper's quarters, not at the top of the lighthouse.

KASTELL DINN

The lifestyle of fishermen in the 19th century

KASTELL DINN **45**
Hameau de Kerlouantec
29160 Crozon
Tel. 02 98 27 26 40
www.gite-rando-bretagne.com
info@gite-rando-bretagne.com

ROOMS AND RATES
Quille en l'air:
75€ for 2 people
Caloge:
100€ for 2 people
Breakfast included
Open year round

Kastell Dinn is a 17th-century longhouse that is typical of the half-rural, half-maritime settlements along the Cap de la Chèvre (Goat's Cape). It is located at the end of a dead end road in the tiny village of Kerlouantec, just 2km from the beach and the town of Morgat. The main house has 5 bedrooms, but others can be found in the garden, where the owners have created living quarters in two boat hulls that were going to be destroyed.

Anchored in the region for many years (Patricia bears the name of a hamlet on Cap de la Chèvre), the owners have thus brought back to life a fisherman's tradition. The géomoniers (seaweed fishermen) sometimes used old boat hulls that could no longer be used on the water to build less costly lodgings.

The result is stunning and gave life to the "Quillle en l'air" (keel up) room, also called the "lover's room", a small stone house whose roof is an upside-down boat hull.

The "Caloge", on the other hand, is a thatched-roof house built in a boat hull.

Other houses with boat-hull roofs, called the "Quilles en l'air", can be found in La Falaise Municipal Campgrounds in Equihen, in the Pas de Calais region. Rue Charles Cazin – 62224 Equihen Plage.
Tel. 03 21 31 22 61. www.camping-equihen-plage.fr, camping.equihen.plage@orange.fr, 8 keels (2 people, 4 people, 5 people). Rates: 55€ to 95€ per night for 2 people depending on the season. Reduced rates for stays of 3 nights or longer: 270€ to 540€ per week for 2 people, depending in the season (400€ to 690€ for 5 people). Open from 1 April to 31 October.

DOMESPACE

A round house to let

DOMESPACE ㊻
Céline Bodéré
Lodonnec
29750 Loctudy
Tel. 06 37 68 19 08
or 09 62 50 48 24
www.amivac.com/2010.asp
afi.bodere@wanadoo.fr

ROOMS AND RATES
House for 8 people:
800€ to 1750€ per week
depending on the season
218m² on 2 floors
Open year round

The Domespace houses are made entirely of wood, and their originality lies in the fact that they can rotate thanks to a system of remotely controlled rotating axles. The houses can thus be turned according to the sunlight, the wind, or even the neighbours!

The first Domespaces appeared in the 1990s, and since then, 130 have been built in France. The one in Loctudy, built in 1997, unfortunately no longer has its rotation mechanism, but it is available to let.

Set back on a 3000m² property near the sea and the Loctudy and Lesconil fishing and boating ports, the house is very well located for those longing to discover the Bigouden region, famous for the women's cone-shaped head-dresses.

The house has 6 rooms, including 4 bedrooms (2 double beds and 4 twin-size beds), a mezzanine, a separate kitchen, a large living- and dining-room with a central fireplace, and 2 bathrooms.

Another Domespace house welcomes guests in the Alps. It still has its rotation system (see p. 231).

KERAGAN ISLAND, KNOWN AS "FORT BLOQUÉ"

Blocked on an island, in a fort...

KERAGAN ISLAND, KNOWN AS "FORT BLOQUÉ" **47**
56720 Ploemeur
Tel. 06 61 04 30 31
www.keragan.com
contact@keragan.com

ROOMS AND RATES
Capacity:
10 to 12 people
(5 people in the watchtower, and 7 in the fort)
Entire island
(fort and watchtower):
2900€ to 5200€ per week depending on the season
Weekend rental possible in the off season

Keragan Island is a 6,000m^2 private island located a few hundred metres offshore. Nicknamed "Fort Bloqué" (Blocked Fort) because of the imposing fortifications built on an islet that becomes inaccessible at high tide, this site is available to let and offers guests a unique experience.

The Fort was built in 1747 on the rocky islet known as "de Keragan" after the English attacked Lorient in 1746, with the purpose of destroying the young New India Company that had been set up there. Completed in 1758, and surrounded by ramparts, it possessed a battery of 4 loaded cannons to ensure the defence of the Port-Louis coast at the mouth of the Laïta River.

Five bedrooms lie within the Fort (which guests enter by crossing the drawbridge) and the watchtower, with its 180° view of the sea.

You can reach the islet by crossing the beach by foot or by 4x4 at low tide. A fisherman welcomes guests, offering them his catch of the day: lobster, sole or bass.

A canoe is at your disposal during high tide if you happen to have forgotten something on the mainland. Upon your return, you'll appreciate the large stone fireplace in the living-room all the more.

PARCABOUT – CHIEN NOIR

Nests in the trees

PARCABOUT – CHIEN NOIR **48**
Le Bois du Grao
56590 Ile de Groix
Tel. 02 97 86 57 61
www.parcabout.fr
contact@chien-noir.fr

ROOMS AND RATES
10 nests
65€ per night (duvet, pillow
and headlamp provided)
Breakfast: 8€ (with fresh-
squeezed orange juice…)
Bring your mobile phone
and travel-light!
Open April to October

GETTING HERE
A 45-minute ferry
ride from Lorient.

Located on Groix Island, Parcabout is a curious trail leading through the trees at heights varying from 2m to 8m over 2000m² of netting, without safety harnesses, at the heart of a forest of 200 California pines.

Outside the park, you can spend the night in spectacular nests hanging from the trees, a creation that the owners have patented. You enter the nests thanks to trampoline nets stretched between the trees and the ground. Inside, nets have been attached near the ceiling to store your belongings, like in old trains.

The nests can accommodate 2 adults, and perhaps 1 or 2 children.

Perched in the nests at 8m or 9m high, you can see the ocean, or even sleep under the stars by rolling up the upper part of the nest.

The Langouste, a small Thaï restaurant on the property, is open for lunch.

THE LIGHTHOUSE OF KERBEL

The only lighthouse in France where guests sleep at the top

THE LIGHTHOUSE OF KERBEL 49
71, route de Port-Louis
56670 Riantec
Tel. 06 08 21 37 74
www.pharedekerbel.com
contact@pharedekerbel.com

ROOMS AND RATES
From April to September,
the entire property
is to let (lighthouse, cottage,
outbuilding, heated pool
and sauna) by week:
1400€ to 2500€ per week
From October to March:
lighthouse rental 450€
(Saturday 10am to Sunday
5pm; or Tuesday 10am
to Wednesday 5pm)
Valentine's Day: 650€
New Year's Day: 700€
Additional night: 100€

It was while reading the auction notices in the Ouest-France newspaper that Daniel became curious to visit the Kerbel lighthouse. When he arrived at the top, he fell in love with the view and decided to buy it.

Contrary to most traditional lighthouses, here guests don't sleep below in the lighthouse-keeper's quarters, but at a height of 25m after climbing 123 stairs. The 360° view of Groix, Lorient and Quiberon Bay, through the large bay windows, is extraordinary.

The charming keeper's house can accommodate 6 people, and Daniel has installed a sauna in the former fire tower, which has been cut and lowered.

DIHAN ÉVASION

One of the pioneers in tree-house accommodation

DIHAN ÉVASION 🌓
Myrian and Arno Le Masle
Kerganlet
56400 Ploëmel
Tel. 02 97 56 88 27
or 06 08 10 05 83
www.dihan-evasion.org
contact@dihan-evasion.org

ROOMS AND RATES
5 tree-houses:
Family-sized cabins
(4/5 people):
120€ to 130€ per night
Njâl (3 people):
130€ to 140€ per night
2 yurts (occupancy
for 1 to 6 people):
80€ to 90€ per night
for 2 people
Caravan:
90€ to 100€ per night
for 2 people
Organic breakfast included
Reduced rates starting
on the second night
Additional person:
30€ to 40€
Gourmet basket meal: 20€
Table d'hôtes: 25€
Cabaret evening
and themed dinner: 35€
Bike rental, sauna and
massages upon request
Open from the beginning
of February to the end
of December (only open
weekends in November
and December)

Myrian and Arno were among the first to open tree-houses to the public on their 62-acre family property in the Morbihan region. Today, 5 tree-houses with Breton names (Nijäl, which means to fly; Pradan – to land; Baman – to be filled with wonder; Heol – the sun; and Folenn – leaf) are available.

Myrian, a horse enthusiast, has also had 2 traditional yurts set up: Djajik (Mongolian for charming place) and Naadam (a national holiday centred on Mongolian archery and equestrian games). The latter was set up in the middle of the horse pastures.

Guests should note that they'll have neither running water nor electricity during their stay so close to nature. A pitcher, candles and a dynamo lamp will be provided.

An old-fashioned gypsy caravan is also available to let. Guests can enjoy several local activities: bird-watching outings, story-telling evenings and kite-surfing on the Quiberon peninsula with Arno.

LA VILLA CHEMINÉE (CHIMNEY VILLA)

A house set on a giant 15-metre high chimney!

LA VILLA CHEMINÉE 🔢
44260 Bouée
Reservations : 06 64 20 31 09
www.uncoinchezsoi.net
contact@uncoinchezsoi.net

ROOMS AND RATES
85€ per night for
1 or 2 people
Open year round

GETTING HERE
by Cordemais

La Villa Cheminée (Chimney Villa) is an extraordinary artistic project designed by Japanese artist Tatzu Nishi for the Estuaire 2009 Nantes-Saint-Nazaire art event. This work of art eventually became permanent and it is now possible to spend the night in it. The artist installed a typical 1970s villa at the top of what clearly resembles a factory smokestack (he took his inspiration from the château de Fer, the largest fossil fuel power plant in France).

Located at the head of Ile de la Nation, the villa has an unrestricted view of the Loire estuary and the rocky Sillon de Bretagne.

The house has a well-equipped kitchen and bathroom on the bottom floor, and a bedroom with a double bed on the upper floor.

A stunning little garden surrounds the house.

> "Un coin chez soi" also offers other original places to stay in Rennes, Nantes and Larmor-Plage.

ACTLIEU

A loft/hotel with only one room

ACTLIEU – LE LOFT ⑤②
11, rue Auguste Brizeux
44000 Nantes
Tel. 06 99 77 00 20
www.actlieu.com
actlieu@orange.fr

ROOMS AND RATES
1 mezzanine bedroom
for 2 people,
equipped kitchen,
bathroom
with Italian-style shower
and separate lavatory
115€ per night,
breakfast included
(at your disposal)
100€ for stays
of 3 nights or more

In the Talensac quarter of Nantes, on a quiet street, in a little building, at the back of a courtyard and in a former artist's studio – that's where you'll find the Loft, a unique place designed by Actlieu (a small company whose ambition is to permit artists to exhibit their work in unusual places). It's something between an art gallery, a conference hall and a hotel.

In this 60m^2 loft decorated in a clean, artistic style, you can ask for the fridge to be stocked, have a caterer deliver your meals or a chef prepare them in the kitchen, or get a massage from a licensed massage therapist.

The site has a 20m^2 garden terrace, complete with palm trees and deckchairs.

Actlieu – the boat: le d'Ô

Actlieu has also converted a former 1930s river boat into an original B&B which, unlike a barge, has large openings to the exterior. At night, a system of blinds and curtains allows you to hide from curious eyes. Indoor and outdoor terrace.

130€ per night for 2 people, breakfast included. Reduced rates for stays of 3 nights or more. Open year round. Quai de Versailles – 44000 Nantes

---

LA VILLA HAMSTER

A giant hamster cage

LA VILLA HAMSTER ⑤⑤
Un coin chez soi
2, rue Malherbe
44000 Nantes
Reservations : 06 64 20 31 09
www.uncoinchezsoi.net
contact@uncoinchezsoi.net

ROOMS AND RATES
99€ per night,
breakfast included
(Nespresso coffee machine,
Mariage Frères tea, hot
chocolate, home-made
jam, butter, milk, fruit
juice and biscuits)
At-home massage:
45€ for 45 minutes
High-speed Internet

Yann Falquerho likes to surprise people. In the smallest house in the city centre of Nantes, a former 18th-century caretaker's house, he decided to design a room in a giant hamster-cage to allow guests to slip into the skin of these little creatures.

A real steel wheel 2m in diameter, identical to that of this little rodent, allows guests to take a morning jog after having spent the night 2.5m above the floor. A metal ladder leads to the bed-cage, where you have to crawl on all fours, just like a hamster entering a tunnel. The wheel can be transformed into a table or a couch.

Yann Falquerho has pushed his idea almost to the limit: he has designed a metal and wood cube which activates a hydraulic system that lets guests quench their thirst, and a feeding dish filled with seeds – they're edible and organic. You'll even find hamster hoods so you can live the experience to the fullest!

> "Un coin chez soi" also offers other original apartments, such as "the underwater cabin of Captain Nemo", Jules Verne's famous hero. Here, guests sleep on a waterbed while listening to sounds of the deep sea. Metal passageways add to the impression of being in a submarine.

PLANÈTE SAUVAGE'S "BIVOUAC ON SAFARI"

Like being in Africa

PLANÈTE SAUVAGE'S "BIVOUAC ON SAFARI" 54
La Chevalerie
44710 Port-Saint-Père
Tel. 02 99 21 19 02
www.planetesauvage.com
info@planetesauvage.com

ROOMS AND RATES
160€ for each adult
130€ for children ages 4 to 14
Reduced rates for groups
(140€ and 110€)
Guided tour of the park
in a 4x4, guide, dinner,
lodging in the bivouac,
breakfast, access to
the park on the following
day and to the Marine
City dolphin exhibit
Open April to November,
depending on the weather

Planète Sauvage is a 320-acre animal park that is home to more than 2000 creatures and 200 animal species. After the last visitors have left, a few privileged guests get to spend the night in the park.

It is also a great way to get close to the giraffes, elephants, bears, wolves, rhinoceroses, hippopotamuses, lions, tigers and antelopes, to name a few.

Surrounded by animals and the howling of wolves, guests dine around a campfire before spending the night in a (comfortable) tent. You'd almost think you were in Africa.

GUEST COMMENTS
"Even in the rain, it was a true change of scenery. I felt like I was in Africa."

LA TROGLO

What if heaven was under ground?

LA TROGLO 🄴
Antoine and Sandrine Paris
2, rue des Sentiers
49700 Doué-la-Fontaine
Tel. 02 41 51 20 27
or 06 11 34 33 95
latroglo@orange.fr

ROOMS AND RATES
1 self-catering
accommodation for 5 people
370€ to 490€ per week
depending on the season
185€ per weekend during
low and middle season

As its name indicates, La Troglo is a troglodytic (cave-dwelling) self-catering accommodation located in Anjou. You enter by taking a small trail that descends 8m under ground, where you'll find a pretty little garden that occupies the farm's former courtyard. This is where guests enjoy their breakfast or spend romantic evenings by candlelight.

From the living-room with a kitchenette, you continue underground to the first bedroom. A tunnel leads to the second bedroom and a lovely shower-room with an Italian-style shower.

Rated 3 ears of corn by Gîtes de France, this site is comfortable and charming.

GUEST COMMENTS

"A voyage to the centre of the earth in this timeless, unreal place."
"An unforgettable moment at the heart of our past."

WHAT IS THE ORIGIN OF THESE CAVE DWELLINGS?

Twenty million years ago, the Faluns sea (an ancient sea during the Tertiary period) covered the entire region. Five million years later, as the sea receded, it left a substratum of shelly limestone. This substratum, from which stone (called falun or grison) was extracted to be used for construction, was also a great place to hide. That is why the local population took refuge there during the Norman invasion and the Vendée invasion during the French Revolution. Eventually, they installed homes there, organizing their entire lives around them. These homes were naturally safe, cool in the summer and warm in the winter, easy to maintain and easy to expand as the family grew.

At the end of the 18th century, two-thirds of the inhabitants of Doué-la-Fontaine thus lived in cave dwellings. When they no longer provided the comfort of modern living, they were abandoned by the inhabitants who preferred to live above ground. Since the beginning of the 1990s, a renewed interest in these dwellings has grown, and many of them have been renovated to reassert the value of this underground heritage.

Doué-la-Fontaine is also known for its production of rose bushes: more than 1 million a year!

DEMEURE DE LA VIGNOLE

A magnificent troglodyte pool

DEMEURE DE LA VIGNOLE ⑤⑥
3, impasse Marguerite
d'Anjou
49730 Turquant
Tel. 02 41 53 67 00
www.demeure-vignole.com
demeure@demeure-
vignole.com

ROOMS AND RATES
11 rooms and suites,
including 4 troglodyte
accommodations
95€ to 148€ for 2 people
Additional person: 28€
Breakfast: 10€
Table d'hôtes available
some evenings
"Les Anges" self-catering
(troglodyte) for 4 people:
800€ to 900€ per week
depending on the season
Open March to November

Located in a 12th-century troglodyte village, the Demeure de la Vignole (17th century) possesses a truly beautiful 2-floor troglodyte room carved entirely out of the rock. In addition, and more importantly (because it's less common), it has a remarkable heated troglodyte pool: carved out of the rock, it is lit by soft lighting whose colour changes thanks to a clever lighting system.

Next to the pool, a former tufa stone excavation room that later served as a wine-pressing house is now home to the fitness room.

The site is very well situated for visiting the region.

ANOTHER UNUSUAL HOTEL **NEARBY**

LE CHAI DE LA PALEINE ⑤⑦

This little hotel located on a beautiful property offers the convivial atmosphere of a wine-producing estate. This site's main point of interest is that breakfast is served in tuns, the large casks where wine was stored. Also a carré d'étoiles® accommodation (see p. 138).
- 12 rooms: 54€ to 79€ for 2 people, breakfast: 5€
- Château La Paleine - 10, place Jules Raimbault
  49260 **Le Puy-Notre-Dame** • Tel. 02 41 38 28 25
- lapaleine@wanadoo.fr • www.paleine.fr

L'AMARANTE

A night for two on a boat

L'AMARANTE 🔵
1 bis, rue des Perrières
37500 Candes-Saint-
Martin (between
Chinon and Saumur)
Tel. 02 47 95 80 85
www.bateauamarante.com
info@bateauamarante.com

ROOMS AND RATES
300€ for 2 people,
all-inclusive (cruise, buffet
dinner and breakfast)

Sometimes called "coches d'eau" (horse-drawn barges) in reference to travellers in the 18th and 19th centuries (in contrast to "coches à terre" or stagecoaches which carried numerous travelers and merchandise), the superb traditional boats L'Amarante and La Belle Adèle now welcome visitors. Although the former can accommodate up to 34 people for a cruise, and the latter up to 26, L'Amarante can accommodate only 2 overnight guests.

Traditionally, the boat casts off at the end of the day for a wonderful one-and-a-half-hour cruise. Viewed from the water, the Saint-Martin Collegiate Church and, later, the château de Montsoreau are impressive indeed. After dinner, the boat berths for the night at the joining of the Vienne and Loire Rivers, and the crew slips away, leaving the lucky couple alone on board. The next morning, the captain delivers breakfast.

Note that there's no shower on board!

TROGLODODO

Charming troglodyte rooms

Troglododo ⑤⑨
Cathy and Alain Sarrazin
9, chemin de Caves
37190 Azay-le-Rideau
Tel. 02 47 45 31 25
www.troglododo.fr
contact@troglododo.fr

Rooms and rates
4 troglodyte rooms,
and another room
in a former pigeon roost
Rates: 60€ to 70€
for 2 people,
breakfast included
20€ for each
additional person

Cool in the summer and relatively warm in the winter, Troglododo's rooms are veritable bedrooms carved out of rock (this isn't always the case for hotels and B&Bs that claim to be troglodyte), the vestiges of an old troglodyte farm of wine growers dating from the 16th and 17th centuries.

Sitting on a hillside facing full south, Troglododo has taken an environmental approach, both in the way it produces its electricity (with solar panels placed on the ramparts of the master's house) and in its use of organic products. Located in the town of Azay-le-Rideau, this magnificent site overlooks the Indre Valley, Honoré de Balzac's famous "Valley of the Lilies". The rooms are independent and open onto lovely flower-filled terraces where you can enjoy your breakfast, weather permitting.

The young and very friendly owners have just added 2 new rooms, "Victoria H" and "Doo Little". Their décor is more modern and mannered (the shower rooms are quite beautiful) than that of the Grand Troglo and Petit Troglo, which are also going to be remodelled.

The Grand Troglo, a 45m^2 suite, can accommodate up to 5 people. It possesses a central fireplace as well as a large dining table.

This is a great address when visiting the châteaux of the Loire valley.

ANOTHER UNUSUAL HOTEL **NEARBY**

Troglodélice ⑥⓪

Along the same lines, a troglodyte room with a large bed and a sofa-bed fit for children. Magnificent shower. Kitchenette at your disposal. Terrace and very beautiful flower-filled garden.

- 60€ for 2 people, breakfast included
  20€ for each additional person
- 3, route de la Vallée du Lys - 37190 Azay-le-Rideau
- Tel. 06 22 83 69 21
- info@troglodelice.com • www.troglodelice.com

LES HAUTES ROCHES

A luxury troglodyte hotel

LES HAUTES ROCHES ❻
86, quai de la Loire
37210 Rochecorbon
Tel. 02 47 52 88 88
www.leshautesroches.com
hautesroches@
relaischateaux.com

ROOMS AND RATES
12 rooms
Troglodyte rooms:
170€ to 280€
Breakfast: 20€

GETTING HERE
The hotel is located
next to Rochecorbon,
which has been granted
the appellation d'origine
contrôlée (label guaranteeing
the origin) of the great
wines of Vouvray
Tours is 8km to the west

With its 12 rooms carved out of the limestone, and its excellent restaurant, the Hautes Roches estate, which opened its doors in 1989, is a stunning place.

The site was first inhabited by the monks of the nearby Marmoutier abbey, before being renovated by the current owner, Philippe Mollard: 18 months of remodelling turned it into the first troglodyte hotel in France. Today, Les Hautes Roches is an ideal home base for visiting the châteaux of the Loire valley.

The caves were first dug to extract the white tufa stone used to build the most famous châteaux of the Touraine region; the monks took refuge in them during the wars of religion. Used from time to time to store wine or grow mushrooms, the caves of the Les Pentes estate were the property of one of the best wine producers of the Vouvray region (from 1855 to 1975), before becoming the warehouse of a liquor supply company.

Carved out of the cliffs, the rooms are truly troglodyte, but equipped with large windows directly overlooking the Loire River. Even without air conditioning, they remain cool during the summer months. A pleasant little outdoor swimming pool has been added on the terraces between the hotel and the Loire.

Don't miss out on a dinner on the terrace, with a view of the Loire. The restaurant of Chef Didier Edon, which has a one-star Michelin ranking, offers delicious regional specialties and wines.

THINGS TO DO NEARBY:

Surprising as it may seem, it is extremely difficult to find a restaurant directly overlooking the Loire River. The RN152, which serves as a dike, almost always acts as a barrier between the water and the different restaurants along its banks. One of the very rare exceptions is the open-air café/ dance hall of Rochecorbon, just a 3-minute drive from the hotel. This restaurant (simple, but good) is open daily in high season. The café, which becomes a dance hall on Thursday and Sunday afternoons, is a great place to experience the popular ambience that creates France's timeless charm. If the people present aren't at the height of their youth, you can nevertheless freely participate in the festivities and dance a little Cha cha cha under the kind watch of the local senior population.

The most pleasant place remains the few tables directly overlooking the water. Unfortunately, you can't enjoy lunch there, but you can enjoy a cocktail before having dinner a few metres away. You can always return for your after-dinner coffee. Taking in the sun with the dance-hall music wafting through the air as you watch the Loire flow by is a rare pleasure.

CHÂTEAU DE RAZAY

A cabin on the grounds of a château

CHÂTEAU DE RAZAY ❷
Michelle Duvivier
37460 Céré-la-Ronde
www.chateauderazay.com
contact@chateauderazay.com
Tel. 02 47 94 38 33

ROOMS AND RATES
2 cabins on stilts:
140€ per night
5 wooden chalets
for 6 people:
300€ for a weekend
and 700€ for a week
Swimming pool and
a tennis court

An evening arrival at the Château de Razay, which is ideally located at the heart of the châteaux of the Loire valley, is quite magical: equipped with a flashlight, Mrs Duvivier, the owner, warmly welcomes you and quickly leads you to the cabins on stilts that stand about 4m above ground. Of course children love it, and even they can easily enter the cabin, thanks to a safe stairway. Depending on the season, you can listen to birds chirping or the wind blowing through the trees, and in autumn you can sometimes hear the troat of a stag – it's quite impressive. The cabins are large and well equipped, but not luxurious. There's just what you need to feel like you're in the trees. Equipped with a lavatory, a shower made entirely of wood, and a sink, the cabins are connected by a footbridge.

The owners, who were looking for a different type of lodging, have also installed Polish chalets on the grounds. Everything is made out of wood, from the floor to the ceiling, including the terrace, the stairs leading to the bedrooms, and the furniture. Breakfast is served in the château's dining-room. The château's grounds are magnificent: in addition to some extremely beautiful trees, you'll find countless animals, such as horses, lamas, and the porcupines that will delight children.

CARRÉ D'ÉTOILES

All the magic of a night spent under the stars

CARRÉ D'ÉTOILES ⑥③
Touraine region
(Chai de la Paleine – see
page 127; La Grangée at
La Chapelle-Blanche-
Saint-Martin)
Saône and Loire region
(La Cabane, DivertiParc
at Toulon-sur-Arroux)
Corrèze
Nièvre
Puy-de-Dôme
Cantal
(Chaux de Revel Estate at
Saint Martin Valmeroux)
Tel. 02 48 77 59 40
www.carre-detoiles.com
info@carre-detoiles.com

ROOMS AND RATES
Beginning
at 85€ per night
for 2 people,
breakfast included
115€ per night for 4 people
An observation kit
is provided for children:
star map, astronomical
telescope,
and astronomy-related
learning games

Over the past few years, the creators of "Carrés d'étoiles" have developed an innovative concept by imagining a 9m² transportable and recyclable cube in which you can sleep under the stars while remaining comfortably indoors.

The cube is topped with a transparent dome that lets guests gaze at the sky from the bed on the mezzanine. The cube also has a bathroom with shower and toilet, a kitchenette, a living-room with a sofa-bed, heating and hot water.

All you have to wish for is a cloudless night sky.

SOUTHWEST

PARC DE LA BELLE

A timeless and magical experience

PARC DE LA BELLE 🔞
Rue Anatole de Briey
86160 Magné
Tel. 05 49 87 80 86
www.parcdelabelle.com
info@parcdelabelle.com

ROOMS AND RATES
12 tree-houses
for 1 to 6 people
111€ per night
for 2 people,
breakfast included.
Complimentary tickets
to the Parc de la Belle
(flower garden)
Family tree-houses:
104€ for 2 people,
31€ each for children
12 or younger,
41€ each for children
over 12,
breakfast included
Dinner basket: 18€ per
adult, includes foie gras,
rillettes (potted meat), goat
cheese, Broyé du Poitou
biscuits, apple juice
and Cabernet wine
(all regional specialties)
Reduced rate offered
for the Vallée des Singes
(Valley of the Monkeys,
around 350 animals
representing 30 species)
Open year round,
closed in January

GETTING HERE
Located 20 minutes
south of Poitiers

Whether you're looking for an adrenaline rush or a family activity to enjoy with your children, at Parc de la Belle (La Belle is a small stream that runs through the park) you'll find what you need to spend an unusual night among the trees.

Standing 4m to 6m above ground, the family cabins are accessible by a staircase and are thus authorized for children as young as 2 years old.

For those looking to get a little higher, the ladder-cabins stand at heights of 9m, 10m or 14m above ground and are accessible by stairs or, for the last 2 metres, by a stepladder (forbidden for children under 12). Finally, more athletic guests can strap on a harness and access the tree-houses located between 10m and 14m above ground.

The tree-houses are equipped with dry toilets; showers are available at the park entrance. Since the tree-houses don't have electricity, you'll be provided with candles, as well as sheets and a harness, if necessary.

To fully enjoy the experience, we suggest that you request a dinner basket for a candlelit dinner high up in the tree-house. That way, you can easily slip into bed after dinner.

The next morning, breakfast is delivered at the base of the tree. You'll just have to hoist it up to the terrace.

LES FOLIES D'AMÉDÉE - LOU FAGOTIN

"A world where nature and childhood memories seem to go hand in hand"

LES FOLIES D'AMÉDÉE -
LOU FAGOTIN 65
Les Moulins
23290 Saint-Pierre-de-Fursac
Tel. 05 55 63 62 18
www.loufagotin.com
loufagotin@wanadoo.fr

ROOMS AND RATES
12 cabins
Rates: 30€ to 40€
per night,
breakfast included
Free for children under 12
Open 15 May to
15 September

Lou Fagotin was originally a small company that had a 20-year-plus history of designing and creating chestnut furniture. Lucien Cassat, the company's founder, wanted to restore the reputation of this wood and, to do so, he worked with several designers (Castelbajac, Garouste). Beyond his business, Cassat wanted to share his love for nature and allow people to rediscover forgotten sensations. So, at the heart of the Vallée des Moulins (Valley of the Mills), he created the Folies d'Amédée (Amédée's Follies).

Hung 2.5m above ground or set on the ground, in an enchanting site close to nature, guests thus sleep in different types of "abricabane" (cabin-shelters): the goat-herder's cabin (built with wood logs), the chrysalis (a straw nest held between 2 tree trunks), the cocoon (hung and covered in cowskin), the beechnut (a kind of den protected by oak trees), or the carambola (shaped like an apple, in the middle of a clearing and equipped with a hammock). All of these playful cabins have one thing in common: they are made of chestnut, and some also have cotton and straw.

As the cabins provide few modern comforts (no electricity or running water), you'll need to bring your own sleeping-bag. Dynamo lamps will be provided for you to see in the dark.

Lou Fagotin's craftsmen also offer introductory courses in furniture-making and the art of rockwork.

If you prefer more comfort, the "Folies d'Amédée" also offers trappers' cabins, traditional self-catering cottages, bungalows and other cabins.

LES ÂNES DE VASSIVIÈRE
(THE DONKEYS OF VASSIVIÈRE)

In the Limousin region, paths have ears

LES ÂNES DE VASSIVIÈRE 66
Yurts on Champseau farm
87470 Peyrat-le-Château
Tel. 05 55 69 41 43
www.anes-de-vassiviere.com
contact@anes-de-
vassiviere.com

ROOMS AND RATES
4 yurts
230€ to 340€ per week
depending on the season,
for 1 to 4 people
Breakfast: 4€ to 6€
For 1 night only: 46€
for 2 people,
breakfast included
Open mid-April
to mid-October
(Booking begins
in December)

The five yurts of "Les Ânes de Vassivière" (the Donkeys of Vassivière) arrived direct from Mongolia by boat, passing from the capital, Oulan-Bator, through China, and finally to Europe. Made according to authentic local tradition, they have a wooden frame covered in several layers of cloth: insulating felt, waterproof canvas and an outer canvas. One of the yurts is especially reserved for cooking and also serves as a shelter when it rains.

The "Ânes de Vassivière" camp is located on a learning farm that houses about 20 donkeys available for family rides through the Limousin mountain. Children love it, and those who tire quickly can rest on the donkey's back.

LA VERGNOLLE

A log cabin on the bank of a pond

LA VERGNOLLE ⑰
23270 Roches
Tel. 05 55 80 81 97
www.lavergnolle.com
bouret.philippe@wanadoo.fr

ROOMS AND RATES
2 four-person log cabins
Week rates: 460€ to 565€
depending on the season
2 days: 195€
3 days: 285€
4 days: 405€
Open year round

"Fustes" are cabins made of untreated round logs positioned on top of one another so as to create a solid, watertight wall. Each trunk, or log, whose bark has simply been removed, retains its shape and curves, which hug the preceding log. The result is a welcoming and unusual house located on the bank of a pond that is perfect for fishing enthusiasts, as the pond is swarming with carp, tench, roach and black bass (for sport fishing).

La Vergnolle possesses two log cabins: the Trapper's Cabin and the Fisherman's Cabin. They each have two bedrooms, a bathroom and lavatory, as well as a large living-room where a wood bar serves as a separation to the kitchen.

Both cabins have a terrace and are surrounded by the peace of an enclosed 3.5-acre tree-filled property.

LA GRANDE SERVE

Silence, the countryside and the charm of gypsy caravans

LA GRANDE SERVE 68
03250 La Chabanne
Tel. 04 70 56 43 18
www.lagrandeserve.com
info@lagrandeserve.com

ROOMS AND RATES
1 two-person caravan,
4 caravans
let in pairs for families
50€ to 70€ per night
for 2 people
depending on the season
320€ to 485€
per week for 2 people
505€ to 710€ per week
for 2 caravans
Bathroom and lavatories
in the old barn
Open from the end of
April to the end of October
(space heaters available)
Weekly rentals only
in the summer

Adriann and Liesbeth came to this little corner of the Monts du Bourbonnais by chance. When Adriann won the Annecy short film award in 2005, they decided to become independent and left the Netherlands, their native country.

Then, they came across a magazine and discovered gypsy caravans. They bought two secondhand gypsy caravan replicas, set them up on a property they had purchased in the Forez region, and turned them into a B&B.

An article in the Dutch press caught the attention of a man who had two caravans, and he offered to exchange them in return for a few weeks' stay.

That's how Liesbeth and Adriann came to own six caravans, five of which are available to let and are set up in three areas of the garden to preserve the privacy of all guests.

The owners kindly offer to deliver bread and pastries each morning as a small, ecological gesture, to keep all the guests from having to drive several kilometres. They also offer organic vegetables from the garden and eggs laid by their own chickens. Otherwise, you can do your shopping in the nearby village, a short 600m walk, but a 3km drive, away.

Situated in the Monts du Bourbonnais, the Grande Serve (which means "pond" in the local dialect) is an ideal starting point for long hikes.

LA HUTTE PERCHÉE

Sleep in a tree-house 9 metres above ground before going skiing

LA HUTTE PERCHÉE 69
Lioran Aventure
15300 Le Lioran
Tel. 06 74 97 40 94
www.lioran-aventure.com
contact@lioran-aventure.com

ROOMS AND RATES
90€ per night for 2 people
(must be at least 14 and
accompanied by an adult)
Breakfast included
Shower in a nearby hotel
Entrance to the hotel's
health-balneotherapy
spa: 10€ per person
Closed in October
and November

La Hutte Perchée is a little tree-house located 9m above ground in the middle of the Accrobranches (tree climbing) course of the Lioran ski resort in the Cantal and Monts d'Auvergne region.

To reach the tree-house, you slip on a helmet and harness (they'll explain how it works) before starting the 4 stages of the course: 3 ladders and a tyrolean traverse. It takes 5 to 10 minutes to reach the top, in the middle of the pines, where the view of the Auvergne volcanoes is magnificent.

The tree-house, a kind of little mountain chalet, is quite comfortable. It is equipped with a thick duvet for the bed, electricity, heating and a dry toilet. You can enjoy breakfast in the tree-house (an electric kettle, tea and coffee are provided – it is recommended that you bring the rest the day before) or in a hotel just a 5-minute walk away, where you can also have a shower.

THE BURON OF NIERCOMBE

A timeless refuge

THE BURON OF NIERCOMBE ⑦
15800 Saint-Jacques-des-Blats
Tel. 06 80 24 23 33
www.niercombe.fr
contact@niercombe.fr

ROOMS AND RATES
Capacity: 4 people
(and 2 people in the annex)
3-day weekend (2 nights)
minimum: 1250€
(350€ for each
additional night)
The rate includes transport
to the buron in a 4x4,
and a kitchen stocked with
enough food for 2 dinners,
a lunch and 2 breakfasts.
Open May to October

The Buron of Niercombe is a former cheese dairy, at an altitude of 1450m, that you reach by taking a 4x4 on a private drive, accompanied by a mountain guide who will come to pick you up on the day of your departure. In the meantime, you'll be able to enjoy the solitude and the countryside's wild beauty – an exceptional experience. The buron is a traditional stone building with a lauze stone roof that is found in mountain pastures. Traditionally in the Auvergne region, the stockbreeders in the valley who own the pastures use them in the summer months. The burons are used to house the cheese-making equipment and to lodge the cheese-makers. Many burons have been abandoned, but some are now being used again, like that of Niercombe. The interior décor is simple, but welcoming. The furniture and flooring are made of wood, and there is a stairway leading down to the kitchen and bathroom below the main room. The water comes from the property's own springs. The Buron of Niercombe, which was built on a ledge more than 300 years ago, overlooks the Cère valley. It provided shelter to shepherds up to the 1940s, but was then left abandoned to the nature of the Monts du Cantal for over 60 years. It took 4 years of restoration work to turn it into this enchanting, timeless place.

Other burons where you can dine or spend the night
The Buron de la Thuillière (or Tuillère) in the village of Thiézac (tel. 04 71 47 06 60), access by car by taking the Curebourse Pass above Vic-sur-Cère. 15 beds in a stable. Meals.
The beautiful **Buron de la Fumade Vieille** (contact Bernard Montimart: 06 71 77 09 04 or 04 71 47 13 64. fvbc@orange.fr). Awarded 3 ears of corn by Gîtes de France. Open April to October.
Buron de la Combe de la Saure, in the village of Brezons. To reserve a table: 04 71 23 04 34. Regional dishes (+/– 16€). No lodging.

MOULINS-GÎTES DU PLATEAU D'ALLY

"Inside, it's small. Outside, it's infinity."

MOULINS-GÎTES DU PLATEAU D'ALLY ⑦
Moulin de Montrome
Moulin de la Meunière
Le Bourg
43380 Ally
Tel. 04 71 07 41 65
(the Loisirs reservation centre, Haute-Loire region)
www.ally43.fr/content/view/17/37/
contact@auvergnevacances.com

ROOMS AND RATES
Weekend (2 nights): 109€
Week: 224€ to 341€
depending on the season
TV, barbecue grill, dishwasher, enclosed field, sheet rental

After the French Revolution, during the first half of the 19th century, countless mills were erected, including the ten windmills of the town of Ally, built around 1820 in local stone. Unlike wooden windmills, the entire body of which can pivot, here, only the cone-shaped roof turns on a circular track. The roof was rotated with a "queue", a long piece of wood attached to a crosspiece on the frame, in order to place the sails in the direction of the wind, or to turn them away when it was time to stop the mill.

On the Ally plateau (1070m above sea level), 3 windmills have been renovated to welcome visitors, and 2 have been transformed into self-catering accommodation: the Moulin de Montrome and the Moulin de la Meunière, both of which can accommodate 2 people.

On the ground floor, a kitchenette allows guests to prepare meals and, on the upper floor, the bedroom lies beneath a very romantic cone-shaped frame. You can hear the wind blow and the birds sing.

The Brantome mill offers the most beautiful view. The other mill is located at the end of a small path, so it is even more tranquil.

The Ally plateau is also home to 26 modern wind turbines, which proves that the location of the old windmills was well chosen.

LES DEUX ABBESSES

A village where each house is a bedroom

LES DEUX ABBESSES ⑫
Le Château
43300 Saint-Arcons-d'Allier
Tel. 04 71 74 03 08
www.lesdeuxabbesses.com
abbesses@relaischateau.com

ROOMS AND RATES
14 rooms
Half-board per day
per person for 2 people,
includes a room for 2,
afternoon tea, dinner,
breakfast, and water from
the mini-bar: 230€ to 330€
Open from Easter to
All Saints Day

The village of Saint-Arcons-d'Allier, located at the start of the Haut-Allier gorges, in the Haute-Loire region, was brought out of oblivion a few years ago thanks to the efforts of a mayor who accepted a hotel project in the hopes of seeing his village live again.

Perched 540m above sea level, the village, which possesses a 12th-century castle adjoining a small Roman church, had been deserted by its inhabitants up to the 1980s.

Today, the Deux Abbesses Hotel (named after Isabeau and Gabrielle Lafayette, whose cloister occupied a part of the castle in the 16th century), fills both the château, where you'll find the reception desk, lounges and the restaurant, and several houses throughout the village.

The entire village was renovated in such a way that you can still imagine what life used to be like here: the alleys connecting the various rooms were rebuilt in the traditional style, and some of the houses have been left untouched.

The room with a canopy bed made from birch tree trunks is a highly prized room, as is the lovely terrace garden offering a view of the valley that allows guests to

relax while remaining hidden from view.

GUEST COMMENTS
"Spending a single weekend in this magical place allowed me to recharge my batteries."

SEEKO'O

The "iceberg" hotel

SEEKO'O **73**
54, quai de Bacalan
33300 Bordeaux
Tel. 05 56 39 07 07
www.seekoo-hotel.com
contact@seekoo-hotel.com

ROOMS AND RATES
45 junior suites ranging
from 27m² to 55m², including
2 rooms with round beds
(rooms with a terrace
and unobstructed view
of the wharf), and a suite
with a "wide-angle"
panoramic view
Rates ranging from 189€
for a junior suite to 380€
for the panoramic suite
20€ for each
additional person
Children 10 or
younger are free
Breakfast: 16€
Large hammam and sauna

The project of the Seeko'o hotel was born in the visionary concept of an inhabitant of the neighbourhood who imagined building a little hotel in the abandoned lot opposite his home. In 1999, he launched his project and the mayor of Bordeaux approved it, under the condition that the hotel be a luxury hotel.

Now, the Seeko'o is a real success. The hotel seems to be planted on the banks of the Garonne River. Inspired by icebergs (the translation of "seeko'o" in the Inuit language), the hotel's modernity is striking, as it is rather rare in Bordeaux, which is better known for its historic city centre, classed as a UNESCO world heritage site.

The bar is open to everyone, including people not staying at the hotel. It has recently started offering cocktails created by grand chefs whose restaurants are located in Bordeaux.

L'ÎLE AUX OISEAUX

A suite in a "tchanquée" cabin

L'ÎLE AUX OISEAUX 🄫
Les Sources de Caudalie
Chemin de Smith Haut-Lafitte
33650 Bordeaux-Martillac
Tel. 05 57 83 83 83
www.sources-caudalie.com
reservations@sources-
caudalie.com

ROOMS AND RATES
600€ to 650€ depending
on the season
Breakfast: 20€ to 22€

Located at the heart of Bordeaux's vineyards, the Sources de Caudalie Hotel possesses an extraordinary suite, called the "Île aux Oiseaux" (Bird Island), the name of an island in Arcachon Bay where one can find "tchanquée" cabins (beach houses on wood poles).

A pontoon leads to the house built entirely of wood and on piles. On the lake, your only neighbours will be the swans – perfect for a romantic night away from it all.

The cabin has recently been fully redecorated by Maison Martin Margiela who has conceived an avant-garde atmosphere (a blend of white, grey and black, with touches of red and trompe l'oeil effects) that is in total contrast to the cabin's exterior.

LES ECONOMIES D'ENEGIE A L'ERE DU RECYCLAGE

Théorie : "Rien ne se perd, rien ne se crée, tout se transforme" *Lavoisier*

Applications possibles :

_ Si j'étais anorexique, je n'aurais pas à payer ma facture d'EDF

_ Si je devenais un être à sang froid, je pourrais chauffer mon appartement à 35°C

_ Si je ne buvais pas d'alcool, ma voiture pourrait consommer plus et donc rouler plus vite

_ Si je ne respirais pas, mes plantes d'appartement seraient plus vertes

_ Si j'étais inactive, je pourrais accélérer la vitesse de calcul de mon ordinateur

_ Si je ne me lavais pas, l'eau du robinet serait buvable

_ Si je ne parlais pas, la radio pourrait fonctionner sans pile

_ Si je dormais sans rêver, je ne paierais pas la redevance télé

LE JARDIN D'HÉLYS-ŒUVRE

A real work-of-art estate

LE JARDIN D'HÉLYS-ŒUVRE **75**
Domaine des Gissoux
Route départementale 705
24160 Saint-Médard-
d'Excideuil
Tel. 05 53 52 78 78
Free entry year round,
daily, 3pm to 7pm
or by appointment
http://lejardindhelys-
oeuvre.fr
jardin.d.helys@wanadoo.fr

ROOMS AND RATES
6 double rooms,
20€ to 60€ per night
Breakfast: 5€
Self-catering accommodation:
320€ to 400€ per week
depending on the season
French "chèques
vacances" accepted
Open year round

In 1995, Alain Piot di Massimo (the father), Moniqa Ray-Bool (the mother), Claude Piot and Lorenzo (the sons) bought the Gissous estate, a 19th-century mansion, and invited artists to express themselves freely on a 32-acre area of the grounds.

The result is frankly stunning. From *in situ* creations to temporary works, the site itself has practically become a work of art.

Today, the mansion welcomes artists and visitors interested in adopting a work of art – the room where they'll stay – for a night, or two, or more.

CHÂTEAU GAUTHIÉ

A true house in the trees

CHÂTEAU GAUTHIÉ 🌀
24560 Monmarvès
Tel. 05 53 27 30 33
www.chateaugauthie.com
château.gauthie@laposte.net

ROOMS AND RATES
1 two-person tree-house and
1 five-person tree-house
Small tree-house:
115€ to 160€ per night,
breakfast included
Large tree-house
(2 to 5 people):
155€ to 250€ per night
depending on the number of
people (2 nights minimum)
Let by the week
in July and August:
1000€ to 1500€ depending
on the number of people
Open from Easter
to 11 November
(heating provided)

Château Gauthié is a family manor located at the heart of the Perigord pourpre region. The tree-house, a little nest for two, stands 8m above ground. Its 25m² include a beautiful terrace and a bathroom with a shower.

Another tree-house standing 5m above ground can accommodate up to five people. Within its 55m², you'll find two bedrooms, a kitchen and a shower.

In the grounds, guests can enjoy the swimming pool and jacuzzi, play a game of petanque or badminton, go fishing in the lake (equipment can be borrowed), or even play a round of croquet in the shade of trees at least 100 years old.

Francette, the proprietor, would also be delighted to show you her garden and very beautiful rose garden.

LA TOULZANIE

A dream of a little house

LA TOULZANIE ⓻
46330 Saint-Martin-Labouval
Tel. 05 65 35 13 65
or 06 82 43 19 18
fau.eliane@wanadoo.fr

ROOMS AND RATES
Self-catering for 2 people
For 1 week:
250€ (April, May
and October),
350€ (June and September),
450€ (July and August)
Open April to October

Thanks to its location on the riverside and against a cliff, La Toulzanie is truly enchanting.

A narrow staircase leads down to the river where you'll find a boat left at your disposal.

In the summer, the morning light reflected in the river is a glorious sight. In the afternoon, the cliff blocks the sun, thus providing the house with a pleasant coolness.

ANOTHER UNUSUAL HOTEL **NEARBY**

LE MOULIN DES GUILLANDOUX ⓼

The Moulin des Guillandoux, a former flour mill turned paper mill, dates back to the 13th century. Long left abandoned, the site, which is listed in the ISMH (Supplementary Inventory of Historic Monuments), adjoins Neolithic troglodyte dwellings, which also recovered their original function when the mill was renovated. After having cleared out the spaces in the rock, the owner opened 2 self-catering accommodations: the grotto and the loft, where an old paper press has been reinstalled. Although the site is not luxurious, it is beautiful.
• Chemin de Guillandoux - 24150 **Couze-et-Saint Front**
• Tel. 05 53 61 71 04
• http://guilllandoux.free.fr • guillandoux@orange.fr
• 2 troglodyte self-catering accommodations: the Grotto (30m^2)
   for 2 people: 350€ to 400€ per week depending on the season
   The Loft (140m^2) for 4 to 6 people: 460€ to 500€ per week depending on the season • Open May to September

L'IMPÉRIAL

One of the most beautiful pigeon roosts in France

L'IMPÉRIAL 🟡
Las Peços Loungos-Bories
82400 Saint-Paul-d'Espis
Tel. 05 63 29 12 61
or 06 71 50 63 60

ROOMS AND RATES
Weekend: 170€ for 2 people
Week: 260€ to 480€
depending on the season
Gourmet package
(3 days/2 nights):
310€ for 2 people,
includes 1 dinner
Open year round

L'Impérial, a pigeon roost located on the grounds of a 5,000m² property, dates from the 18th century. Left abandoned, it was bought by the current owners who had watched the frame of its roof slowly collapse. Photographs taken before the full collapse, along with the remaining pieces of wood, made it possible for an experienced carpenter to reconstruct a roof frame identical to the original, a frame that you can admire from the bedroom on the upper floor. The site has been furnished with all modern comforts and can accommodate 2 people. On the ground floor, you'll find a kitchen, and on the next floor, there is a living-room and a shower-room. Each floor measures 16m², which provides a spacious feeling accentuated by the imposing height of the ceilings. Its dimensions make it one of the largest pigeon roosts in the region, which is home to quite a few. From November to March, Patrick Dumontier, who owns a restaurant in Dunes, offers dining in the pigeon roost. Your hostess, who will do everything in her power to provide the best quality service, will set the table, serve the dinner, and then leave you to enjoy an evening for two.

LE MOULIN DU PÉTO

A mill with a view

LE MOULIN DU PÉTO ⑧⓪
Larroque-sur-l'Osse
32100 Condom
Reservations : Loisirs
accueil Gers
Tel. 05 62 61 79 00
www.gers-tourisme.com
contact@gers-tourisme.com

ROOMS AND RATES
Capacity: 2 to 3 people
Rates ranging from 190€
per week in the low
season to 390€ per week
in the high season
Open April to All Saints' Day

The lovely stone Péto windmill was once part of the property of the Château de Beaumont sur l'Osse, the former château of the Marquis de Montespan. Located on the hill opposite the château, the mill dominates the Osse valley and offers a 360° view.

Originally, there was a large number of mills, but most of them were demolished. This was one of the first to be renovated and it still has its sails. Surrounded by a shaded lawn perfect for a barbecue, the mill has 4 floors connected by a very beautiful staircase.

The owners, who are Armagnac producers, will happily take you on a guided tour of their property and offer a tasting.

CASTELNAU DES FIEUMARCON

Unlike anything else

CASTELNAU DES FIEUMARCON ⑧⑨
Lagarde
32700 Lectoure
Tel. 05 62 68 99 30
www.lagarde.org
office@lagarde.org

ROOMS AND RATES
13 houses
and 4 B&B rooms
Self-catering accommodation:
1000€ to 3000€ per week
B&B: 100€ per night
for 2 people
(2 nights minimum)
Breakfast extra
It is possible to book
the entire site: rates
upon request
Open year round

Le Castelnau is a small, 13th-century fortified village overlooking the Gascony countryside. In 1975, the village was in ruins. An enthusiast bought the homes one by one, planning to reconstruct the village according to the Venice Charter, an international charter on the conservation and restoration of monuments and sites.

Today, 16 charming houses are available for let, as self-catering accommodation or as B&B. Some can accommodate 2 to 3 people, while others can comfortably hold 8 to 9 guests.

At the entrance to Le Castelnau, a tennis court on the "patus" (the name given to land belonging jointly to all the terraced houses) and a swimming pool below the ramparts are open to guests.

> The owner of Le Castelnau des Fieumarcon is also the proprietor of Lisbon's gorgeous Palacio Belmonte, which is probably the best luxury, privately-owned hotel of the Portuguese capital. The Ricardo Reis room, with its terrace overlooking the Tage River and 17th-century azulejos panels, is particularly pleasing.

LES CABANES DU MENOY

A family cabin in the trees

LES CABANES DU MENOY 82
Hubert Avantanéo
68, chemin du Menoy
40550 Léon
Tel. 06 71 72 99 68
www.lescabanesdumenoy.com
lescabanesdumenoy@orange.fr

ROOMS AND RATES
2 tree-houses
Léotine (2 to 6 people):
102€ to 138€ per night
for 2 people depending
on the season
and the length of stay,
breakfast included
Additional person: 42€ to 55€
Léonie (2 people):
120€ to 162€ per night
depending on the season
and the length of stay

Perched around an oak tree more than 100 years old, at a height of 6.8m, the Léonie tree-house can be reached by climbing up a spiral staircase leading to a large terrace, where you'll find comfortable chairs and an unrestricted view of the Landes forest, a pond and a prairie.

Léotine, the other tree-house, stands on piles at 4m above ground. A family-size cabin, it can accommodate 6 people, which is rather rare. The parents' room is on the first level, as is the bathroom. The children climb up to the tower, at a height of 7m, where they sleep in bunk-beds.

In the morning, a breakfast basket will be delivered at the base of the tree.

GUEST COMMENTS

"To sleep in a tree and listen to it creak. A warm welcome."
"A haven of peace where time seems to stand still, and where we take the time to hear the spirits of nature and to listen to our hearts."

DJÉBELLE – THE B&B BARGE

"The Adour River as far as the eye can see."

DJÉBELLE 🕸
Opposite 17, quai de Lesseps
64100 Bayonne
Tel. 05 59 25 77 18
www.djebelle.com
contact@djebelle.com

ROOMS AND RATES
2 rooms
140€ for 2 people
Breakfast composed entirely
of homemade goods: 8€
Closed November to April,
with some exceptions
Reservation required
The owners organize
"open barge" days
with an art exhibit
and reception.
By invitation only.

Located on the banks of the Adour River, at the site of the former port of Bayonne, the Djébelle barge recently came back to life thanks to the care of Isabelle and Patrice Bellon. Found as a scrap heap in an abandoned depot in Bordeaux, this English barge at least 100 years old is believed to have carried ammunition across the Channel during the Normandy landings.

The long and difficult restoration of the boat was supported by the town hall, which was looking to enliven the riverside. Isabelle and Patrice thus turned their residence into an elegant place, where guests are welcomed in a warm and refined manner. In the summer, breakfast is served hidden from view on the terrace made of teak that provides a plunging view of the river, watchtower and a branch of the Nive River. Two rooms are reserved for guests, one at each end of the boat.

The chambre des îles (Island room), which has a boat-themed décor, occupies the former bargee's cabin. Spacious and built entirely of wood (even the porthole blinds are in wood), it has a small, private terrace with teak deckchairs. The bathroom has been installed in the wheelhouse, where the magnificent helm serves as a towel rack. The

chambre Riad, at the front of the boat, has a Moroccan-style décor with a platform bed and ceramic tile shower.

This barge is a beautiful, intimate and elegant place for lovers to contemplate a sunset or a misty early morning.

THE LEGORDIA BORDA CABINS

Guest cabins in the trees

THE LEGORDIA BORDA CABINS 84
Frédéric and Sue Jeanniot
Route de l'Artzamendi
64250 Itxassou
Please call only in the
morning: 05 59 29 87 83
www.legordia.fr

ROOMS AND RATES
3 tree-houses
Rates ranging
from 100€ to 130€
for 2 people (children: 30€)
Traditional breakfast: 7€
Dinner: 18€
Champagne and candlelight
for your arrival,
by reservation: 50€

A few years ago, Frédéric Jeanniot, a set designer, decided to leave Paris and his stressful life. He moved in with Sue on her family's sheep farm near Itxassou. At a picnic, Frédéric watched the children climb in the trees and was hit with a crazy idea: to build cabins in the trees, but for adults. Five months later, the first tree-house was completed; two others followed.

The 3 tree-houses were built following the same design and according to certain rules: no nails or screws in the trees, no cut branches, and no changes to the trunk. Each tree-house has a shower fed by spring water, a toilet and heating. They also have a terrace with deckchairs and a table to enjoy the breakfast or dinner prepared by Sue.

All of the products she serves are organic or farm-raised and are exclusively from the region. For breakfast, a basket is hoisted up to the tree-house. Sue also prepares baskets for the evening meal according to her tastes and the season.

You should note that there is a high demand for this little paradise, so you must reserve early.

LA CABANE DES MÉSANGES BLEUES

A terrace 12m above ground

LA CABANE DES
MÉSANGES BLEUES (85)
Near Trie sur Baïse (65)
Reservations: Loisirs
Acceuil Gers
Tel. 05 62 61 79 00
www.gers-tourisme.com
contact@gers-tourisme.com

ROOMS AND RATES
1 tree-house
150€ for 2 or 3 people,
breakfast included
15€ for each
additional person
Dinner basket: 25€
Open year round

After business school and a job that just didn't fit, the designer and owner of this tree-house unlike any other decided to make a change and returned to the family farm, which dates back to the 16th century.

Since he knew that there were already numerous tree-houses in France, he decided to build a different one that anyone could enjoy: tall and short, young and old, the able-bodied and the physically-challenged.

As paying for professional construction was beyond his means (he wanted a large, 40m² cabin), he naturally set to work himself, equipped with his tractor, pulleys, chainsaw, and a lot of determination. After six months of work, the tree-house was finished. Resting on eight large oak trees, the cabin is surrounding by solitude and has two double beds, with the possibility to add an extra bed, so that it can comfortably accommodate up to six people. A small, equipped kitchen allows guests to prepare meals.

A bridge leads to the 40m² terrace that stands 12m above ground.

In collaboration with Patrice, the neighbouring farm/inn prepares delicious and copious dinner baskets.

LE PIC DU MIDI

"There is no one who was born under an unlucky star.
There are just people who don't know how to read the stars."

LE PIC DU MIDI **86**
65200 La Mongie
Tel. 0825 00 2877, Monday
to Friday (office hours)
www.picdumidi.com

ROOMS AND RATES
8 rooms
Capacity: 19 people
199€ per person
or 299€ for 2 people,
includes round-trip
transportation
on the cable-car, dinner,
room, breakfast,
professional guide,
and the various tours
Payable by cheque
to the order of the "Trésor
Public" (it's not every day
that you'll pay the State
to spend the night!)
at the time of reservation
Sheets, duvet and
towels provided
Sink in the room.
Showers and lavatory
in the corridor
Parking at La Mongie
(restricted parking
in the winter)
Open during
the Christmas holidays,
the February holiday,
Easter holidays,
all summer long,
and all weekends,
so approximately
240 nights a year.

Since the summer of 2006, it has been possible to spend the night at the summit of the famous Pic du Midi and live a truly extraordinary experience.

Although the rooms are purposefully rather sparse so as to accentuate the incredible human adventure of the Pic du Midi (the rooms are those normally used by researchers), they all have an unrestricted view of the Pyrenees, which, in addition to the site's unique ambience, more than compensates for any eventual discomfort.

After arriving by cable-car in the late afternoon (before 5pm–6pm from June to September), guests visit the site and then enjoy a cocktail while watching the grandiose spectacle of the sunset, at 2877m above sea level. Next comes dinner (regional specialties) before the long-awaited observation of the stars and night sky. A professional guide is present to lead guests up to the Charvin dome which is equipped with a 400mm telescope. In the morning, after watching the sun rise over the Pyrenees, guests can visit the domes in the scientists' quarters, the only time when they are open to the public.

Don't forget to bring very warm clothes (ski cap, gloves, good shoes, fleece jacket, windbreaker) so you can participate in the outdoor activities under good conditions. At this height, it can turn cold quickly, regardless of the season.

The summit of the Pic du Midi became a site for observation and scientific study at the beginning of the 18th century. Construction of the observatory began in the 1870s and was completed in 1882. The first cable-car was installed in 1952. Although the government considered closing the observatory in 1994, the Midi-Pyrenees region took action and renovated the site.

INDIAN TEEPEES

An incredible view of the cirque de Gavarnie

LES TIPIS INDIENS **87**
Quartier Saussa
65120 Gèdre
Tel. 06 15 41 33 29
www.tipis-indiens.com
info@tipis-indiens.com

ROOMS AND RATES
4 teepees for 4 to 6 people
350€ to 540€ per week
depending on the season
85€ for 1 night,
140€ for 2 nights,
195€ for 3 nights
Weekly rental
only in July and August
2 stone barns are also
available as self-catering
accommodation:
beginning at 490€ per week
Open 1 May to
the beginning of October

At 1300m above sea level right in the middle of the countryside, among free-ranging dwarf goats that children adore, the Indian teepees can comfortably hold 4 people (or up to 6 if you squeeze in close) and offer an exceptional view of the cirque de Gavarnie. Part of the Parc Naturel des Pyrénées (Pyrenees National Park), the Gavarnie is a natural glacier-type cirque that has been classed as a UNESCO world heritage site since 1997.

A sheep farm full of character houses the kitchen and sanitary facilities, which are shared by the guests of the 4 teepees.

Numerous hiking trails pass nearby.

GUEST COMMENTS

"Just for one night, it was a little short but we loved it! A magnificent setting, warm welcome, perhaps we'll come back for another visit – so, see you soon!"

"Vacation in a teepee, a pleasurable abundance of tranquility and oxygen at an altitude of 1300m, and with an exceptional view of the Gavarnie. The quality of Francis' welcome equalled that of his campsite (4 stars)."

BELREPAYRE AIRSTREAM

A true change of scenery

BELREPAYRE AIRSTREAM **88**
09500 Mirepoix
Tel. 05 61 68 11 99
www.airstreameurope.com
info@airstreameurope.com

ROOMS AND RATES
9 trailers
90€ to 160€ per night,
for 2 to 4 people
depending on the season
Reduced rates for stays
of 3 nights or longer
Can be rented by the week
Possible to rent a parking
space if you have
your own trailer or camper
more than 30 years old
Sheet and towel rental
Jacuzzi, massages
Open from the end of April
to the end of September,
by reservation only

With its magnificent view of the Pyrenees, the hillside campsite of Perry and Coline, the charming proprietors of the Belrepayre farm, has become the European capital for the owners of Airstream trailers. There wouldn't have been such a revival of these trailers, the most elegant form of transportation in the USA from 1950 to 1970, if it weren't for Perry, a restoration expert. Kept in perfect condition, these trailers are in high demand by those looking for an original, retro experience or by film crews.

If you're a disco fan, don't miss the Apollo lounge, the bar of one of the restored Airstream trailers, which becomes the main attraction in the summer, when Perry organizes movie nights and shows. With a little luck, he'll be behind the turntables with his superb collection of 1950s–1970s vinyl records and his son, Coréo, will do a few magic tricks.

The Airstream trailers are fully equipped for cooking. They each have an awning or parasol, a barbecue grill, an outdoor table and chairs, and deckchairs. In the camp, you'll also find a little stand where you can buy staple goods: fresh bread, croissants and ecological specialties from nearby farms. The camp also has ping-pong tables and a football table. Guests can also enjoy a red ciderwood whirlpool bath or a massage in the Mongolian yurt.

PÉNICHE KAPADOKYA

A guaranteed stress-reliever

PÉNICHE KAPADOKYA 89
Écluse de la Méditerranée
11400 Le Mas Saintes Puelles
Tel. 04 68 23 46 71
or 06 86 95 71 36
www.enpeniche.com
kapadokya@wanadoo.fr

ROOMS AND RATES
Capacity:
6 to 9 people (possibly 11)
3 cabins
3 B&B rooms
"On the quay":
70€ per cabin,
for 1 or 2 people,
with shower, sink, lavatory
and breakfast included
Self-catering: entire barge:
from 450€ for a weekend
(2 nights) for 6 to 8 people
(630€ for 9 to 11 people)
to 1000€ for a week
for 6 to 8 people
(1400€ for 9 to 11 people)
Table d'hôtes:
25€ per person, all-inclusive
It is possible to sail the
barge as an optional extra
Bicycles available for loan
Open year round

The owners of the Kapadokya barge didn't arrive here by chance: Nathalie is from Toulouse and Philippe, who is originally from Normandy, used to work as a lock-keeper.

After 6 years of work to transform the barge (which earned the name Kapadokya as a reminder of their numerous trips to Cappadoce, Turkey), it was finally ready to welcome up to 11 guests.

Located in the middle of the countryside, near the famous Not Frères pottery, this Dutch barge was built in Belgium in 1939. It is 30m long and 4.6m wide.

If you reserve the entire barge, you can sail it for a few hours or for the day and pass through a few locks while living according to the slow rhythm of the Midi canal.

CLOS DU MOULIN

Two authentic caravans at the heart of the Minervois region

CLOS DU MOULIN **90**
La Bohême and Lachodrom
Frédérique and
Jacques Buffiere
34, route de l'Aven
11160 Villeneuve-Minervois
Tel. 04 68 26 37 16
www.closdumoulin.net
info@closdumoulin.net

ROOMS AND RATES
2 caravans for 2 people
2-night minimum: 75€ per
night, breakfast included
From 380€ per week in
the off season to 450€
per week in July and
August (as self-catering,
breakfast not included)
Open year round (closed
mid-February to mid-March)
From December to early
February, stays organized
around the theme of
"truffles", a regional
specialty, are offered

Few caravans from the beginning of the 20th century have survived because of an Indian custom of burning the caravans of the dead. The Clos du Moulin succeeded in recuperating two of them.

The first is a 1920s caravan previously owned by fairground people from Prague. It still has its original oiled oak woodwork and bevelled mirrors.

The second, more bohemian-style caravan dates from the 1950s and has been named "Lachodrom", which is Romany for "bon voyage". In fact, these two caravans form a mini-campsite: the living room and bedroom are in one caravan, while the bathroom and kitchen are in the other.

If the caravans have already been reserved, you can stay in one of the three rooms available in the architect house built in the 1950s. They have been decorated by the proprietors, former art gallery owners who are contemporary art and travel enthusiasts.

PÉNICHE LÔDELÀ

A self-catering 1930 barge

PÉNICHE LÔDELÀ 🟤
Écluse de l'Évêque
11800 Villedubert
Tel. 06 82 09 98 75
www.penichelodela.com
hudroulers@voila.fr

ROOMS AND RATES
Self-catering
with 3 cabins for 2 people
From 536€ per week
during the low season
to 1098€ per week
during the high season
Price includes service charges
and 2 mountain bikes
Sheet and towel rental:
5€ per person
Open April to October

When Hugues Droulers fell in love with the Canal du Midi, he decided to buy a barge and live there. Since its size wasn't adapted to that of the Canal's locks, the Maryvonne (the barge's former name), which had served to transport grain in Belgium and northern France, had to be shortened by 10m.

Today, it offers original and comfortable self-catering accommodation, including a well-equipped kitchen as well as a very pleasant shaded terrace.

SOLONGO

Mongolian for "rainbow"

Solongo ②
La Garrigue
34360 Pardailhan
Tel. 04 67 97 18 08
or 04 67 25 36 65
www.camping-solongo.com
solongo5@hotmail.fr

ROOMS AND RATES
Yurt (1 to 6 people):
75€ to 85€ per night
depending on the season,
or 350€ to 400€ per week
1920 caravan
(2 adults and a small child):
60€ to 70€ per night
or 280€ to 330€ per week
depending on the season
Gypsy caravan
(2 adults and 2 children):
55€ to 60€ per night
or 240€ to 280€ per week
Kitchen available
for these accommodations
Blankets provided
Sheet rental available
Swimming pool
and Qi gong sessions
every morning,
horse-riding
Breakfast: 5€
Table d'hôtes: 17€
Open April to mid-November

The Solongo Farm is located in the Haut Languedoc region, between the sea and the mountains at an altitude of 600m. Its owners define themselves as "travellers in search of non-settlement". Two Mongolian yurts, a 1920 caravan, and a gypsy caravan welcome guests on this original campsite.

For younger guests, a Tibetan tent has been set up for games, and Pédro the donkey can take them for rides on marked trails.

In the evening, the open-air café proposes regional and international specialties.

Products from the farm are also for sale.

L'APPART DES ANGES

A barge full of charm, on the Canal du Midi

L'APPART DES ANGES ㉓
Péniche "Les Anges d'Eux"
Canal du Midi
34420 Cers
Tel. 04 67 26 05 57
or 06 11 11 05 87
www.appartdesanges.com
contact@appartdesanges.com

ROOMS AND RATES
3 rooms
105€ to 125€ per night
for 2 people,
depending on the season
and length of stay,
brunch included
2-night minimum rental;
weekly rental
in July and August
Gourmet basket:
55€ for 2 people,
everything from
the cocktails
to the after-dinner liqueur,
décor included!
Open from Valentine's
Day (14 February)
to the end of October

Manufactured in Germany in 1923, Christophe and Jean-Philippe's barge was given to the Allied forces by the Germans as compensation after the war. Today, the barge is home to three nicely decorated bedrooms. Jean-Philippe, a member of Air France's flying personnel, took advantage of his foreign travels to bring back nautical fixtures, such as portholes from old steamships found in depots in Bombay, or plumbing from China that gives the boat a unique atmosphere.

Cabin number 3 has the distinctive feature of possessing a bathtub as well as a bay window at water level opposite the bed – all the better to admire the waves from the moment you awake.

Guests can go on bike rides (the owners will happily loan you bikes) along the nearby towpaths and through the neighbouring vineyards. There are beaches only 10 minutes away, as this part of the Canal du Midi is the closest to the coast.

ANGLETERRE

Amsterdam
PAYS-BAS

Londres

ALLEMA

Douvres
Dunkerque   Vers Bruges
Calais   Vers Gand   Bruxelles
Boulogne-   Lille   Vers Tournai   BELGIQUE
sur-Mer   Vers Bruxelles

Bournemouth
Weymouth
Portsmouth
MANCHE
Abbeville   Arras
Amiens   St-Quentin   Cambrai   Charleville-   Vers Bouillon   Vers Luxembourg
Mézières

Cherbourg-
Octeville
CHANNEL
ISLANDS
Le Havre   Rouen   Beauvais   Laon   Reims   Metz
Caen   Evreux   Cergy-   Châlons-   Nancy
Saint-Lô   Pontoise PARIS en-Champagne Bar-le-Duc
Granville   Alençon Versailles Nanterre   Épinal
St-Malo   Chartres Créteil Troyes Chaumont   Mulho
Saint-   Evry Melun   Vesoul   Belfort
Brieuc   Le Mans   Sens   Dijon   Besancon
Brest   Laval   Montargis Auxerre
Quimper   Rennes   Orléans   Lons-
Vannes   Angers   Blois   Bourges   Nevers   le-Saunier   S
Belle-Ile   Saumur Tours   Genève
Nantes   Châteauroux   Moulins   Mâcon   Vers M
Ile de   Vichy Roanne Bourg- Annecy 103
Noirmoutier   La Roche-   Montluçon   en-Bresse
Ile d'Yeu   sur-Yon   Poitiers   94 97 95   Chambéry
Ile de Ré   Niort   Guéret   98 63
La Rochelle   Limoges   96   100 101 105
Rochefort   Clermont-   Lyon 102 106
Ile d'Oléron   Saintes   Angoulême Tulle Ferrand   99 104 107 Grenoble
OCÉAN   Périgueux Brive-   Saint-Etienne   108   111
ATLANTIQUE   Bergerac la-Gaillarde   Le Puy-   112 113
Bordeaux   en-Velay Valence   Gap
Cahors   Rodez   109
Agen   110   Digne-
Montauban Albi   114   les-Bains
Bayonne   Pau   Tarbes   Toulouse   Nîmes   115 121 116 117
Carcassonne Béziers   122 120 118 63
Foix   Narbonne   123
124 119   126
Perpignan   Marseille 125 Toulon 129
127
ESPAGNE   ANDORRE   MER MÉDITERRANÉE

0   50   100   150

SOUTHEAST

LES CADOLES DE LA COLLINE DU COLOMBIER

Spectacular modernist cocoons

LES CADOLES DE LA COLLINE
DU COLOMBIER 94
La Colline du Colombier
71340 Iguerande
Tel. 06 03 58 30 45
www.troisgros.fr
la-colline-du-colombier@
troisgros.com

ROOMS AND RATES
3 cadoles
Suites for 2 people
2-night minimum
250€ per night

Iguérande's cadoles (named after the old cabins generally built of dry stone that once sheltered wine growers in Burgundy) are spectacular houses on piles, built on a hillside. One of these 3 contemporary homes is suspended in the air; the second, a terrace, fits snugly between two 100-year-old oak trees, and the third is shaded by an apple tree. Guests can live comfortably in all three, since each one is furnished with a large bed, bathroom, small kitchen and a spacious Zen-style living-room that opens onto a balcony overlooking the natural surroundings. The bedrooms are designed like cocoons. Woven hemp covers the ceiling and walls, which seem to blend together to give an incredible effect. This 100% ecological project was conceived by Marie-Pierre and the famous Michael Troisgros, with the help of the no less famous architect Patrick Bouchain. A former adviser to French politician Jack Lang, Bouchain represented France at Venice's Architecture Biennale in 2006. He designed the Zingaro equestrian theatre in Aubervilliers and the "Lieu Unique" in Nantes. Here, the property is also home to an inn housed in a former stable, called "Le Grand Couvert", but you can always go another 15km and dine at Michael Troisgros' gourmet restaurant (3 Michelin stars) in Roanne.

LE PARADIS DE MARIE

A caravan for two at Saint-Amour

LE PARADIS DE MARIE 🍇
Marie and Stéphane
Lefaucheux
Les Ravinets
71570 Saint-Amour-Bellevue
Tel. 03 85 36 51 90
www.laroulottedemarie.com
contact@
laroulottedemarie.com

ROOMS AND RATES
95€ per night,
breakfast included
2-night minimum
Open April to the
end of October

At the heart of the Mâconnais and Beaujolais regions, in the lovely village of Saint-Amour (Amour is French for "love"), Marie and Stéphane have installed a caravan on their property. It's full of warm colours, and the bathroom seems to have come straight from the turn of the century with its magnificent lion's-claw bathtub (a luxury in a caravan!). In front of the caravan, a wood terrace with chairs, a parasol and cushions invite guests to rest after visiting local landmarks (such as Cluny Abbey or the Roche de Solutré) – and the regional vineyards, of course!

We suggest dining at the wonderful restaurant L'Auberge du Paradis located just a short distance away.

LA FERME DE LA SOURCE

Yurts on a hillside

La Ferme de la Source 96
Anne-Marie and
Charles Frénéa
Lieu-dit Lupé
42155 St Jean-St-Maurice
Tel. 04 77 63 77 63
www.lafermedelasource.com
contact@
lafermedelasource.com

ROOMS AND RATES
2 yurts: Orgo and Natschka
20m² yurt (4 people):
60€ for 2 people,
breakfast included;
100€ for 2 nights
27m² yurt (6 people):
70€ for 2 people,
breakfast included;
130€ for 2 nights
Price for 2 nights for a family
with 2 children: 160€
Additional person:
15€ per night,
breakfast included
Hammam and jacuzzi:
20€ for 2 people

La Ferme de la Source (Spring Farm), an old family vineyard renovated to accommodate guests, is located in the gorges of the Loire River, in an exceptional setting. Its nature and tranquility make it a perfect spot for focusing on one's well-being, the concept around which Anne-Marie and Charles have developed their idea.

As traditional B&B bedrooms can't suitably accommodate a family, they have set up two yurts on a hilly part of their property that provides a magnificent view of the Loire River and the surrounding countryside. The yurts bear the names of the young people who came to install them and are furnished in part with very colourful Mongolian furniture.

The sanitary facilities are located in the owners' house, as are the hammam and jacuzzi (outdoors, also open in the winter), the access to which is organized to respect the privacy of each family.

Breakfast is served in a basket at your requested time, to be enjoyed in the yurt (hot drinks, brioche, crêpes). In the summer, an outdoor kitchen is at the disposal of all yurt guests.

Anne-Marie also offers massages and anti-stress sessions.

THINGS TO DO NEARBY

The farm is located near Saint-Jean-Saint-Maurice-sur-Loire, a medieval village on the Compostela pilgrimage route that possesses several beautiful monuments: medieval keep, castle ruins, medieval city gates and ramparts, old homes, a church and an old Benedictine priory.

LES ROULOTTES DE LA SERVE

Stars in a caravan

LES ROULOTTES DE LA SERVE ❼
Pascal and Pascaline Patin
La Serve
69860 Ouroux
Tel. 04 74 04 76 40
www.lesroulottes.com
ppatin@free.fr

ROOMS AND RATES
50€ to 60€
for 2 people,
breakfast included
(additional 3€
to 5€ for heating)
Gourmet meal baskets
available upon request
Open 1 April to the
end of October

Nestled in the Beaujolais hills at an altitude of 700m, Les Roulottes de la Serve are installed on the property of a very beautiful renovated farm. These authentic gypsy caravans have been entirely restored in the spirit of the period.

The lover's caravan, for two, is a little jewel of 1950s sculpted wood, with rugs and armless chairs.

After a lot of work, the 1920s carousel caravan has become a charming place. It has a living-room and can accommodate up to 4 people. A door isolates a small bedroom, perfect for children, from the rest of the caravan.

The last caravan, the star caravan, dates from the end of the 19th century. It owes its name to the multitude of little lights that illuminate its ceiling.

THE AIRSTREAM TRAILER OF LA CROIX DU PY

Spend the night in a 1970s trailer

THE AIRSTREAM TRAILER
OF LA CROIX DU PY ⑨⑧
Florence and Patrick Vacher
La Croix du Py
69430 Avenas
Tel. 04 74 04 76 92
or 06 85 95 06 83
www.croixdupy.com
croisdupy@orange.fr

ROOMS AND RATES
60€ for 2 people,
breakfast included
10€ for each
additional person
Children 2
and younger are free
Child: 5€

In addition to her two other more traditional rooms, a few years ago Florence installed a guest-room in a superb vintage trailer (1973) from Canada.

Although the period décor is impeccable (there's even a bathroom with a bath), the size of the bed is a bit small (only 1.2m wide).

The trailer can also accommodate one or two young children on a period sofa bed.

Florence's husband, Patrick, offers dune-buggy rides along forest paths and through vineyards.

ARTELIT

Renaissance guest chambers

ARTELIT 🌐
Frédéric Jean
16, rue du Bœuf
69005 Lyon
Tel. 04 78 42 84 83
or 06 81 08 33 30
www.dormiralyon.com
artelit@dormiralyon.com

ROOMS AND RATES
Pink Tower:
100€ to 190€ per night,
depending on the season
1565 Suite:
130€ to 250€ per night,
depending on the season

Renowned photograph and art enthusiast Frédéric Jean has opened two Renaissance guest chambers in the buildings surrounding the courtyard of the Tour Rose (Pink Tower), which houses his art studio, at the heart of the Saint-Jean quarter, classed as a UNESCO world heritage site.

The two rooms are entirely furnished in the Renaissance style and have been decorated by different artists, whose works can be purchased.

Breakfast (included) is served in an original manner at the best pastry shop in the neighbourhood, La Marquise, in the Maison du Chamarier, a 16th-century Renaissance palace.

COLLÈGE HOTEL

Just like at school...

COLLÈGE HOTEL 🏅
5, place Saint-Paul
69005 Lyon
Tel. 04 72 10 05 05
www.college-hotel.com
contact@college-hotel.com

ROOMS AND RATES
39 rooms
(air conditioning, LCD TVs,
shower or bath),
panoramic view of the city,
terrace, private car park, wi-fi
Open year round
115€ to 145€ per night
Breakfast: 12€

It took 3 years of antique-hunting for Jean-Luc (who is also the designer and former owner of the Cour des Loges) to recreate the astonishing ambience of the Collège Hotel.

Installed in the only Art Déco building of the Vieux Lyon quarter, classed as a UNESCO world heritage site, the Collège Hotel pays homage, as its name indicates (collège is French for "secondary school"), to our childhood and adolescent dreams, the ones we had while seated at our schoolroom desks, admiring maps of the world and letting our minds wander.

Nothing has been forgotten: desks, chairs, paintings, chalkboards, old books and a classroom, with which high technology, comfort and design now mix.

At the entrance is a plinth with a 1914 pommel horse that used to stand in the gym of the Lycée Royal de Versailles (Versailles Royal High School).

There are also the vintage 1960s refrigerators from which "boarders" could freely take a non-alcoholic beverage while reflecting on the quotations written on the corridor walls.

The hotel's 130 windows light up in a surprising manner at night thanks to an extraordinary play of lights.

COUR DES LOGES

Spend the night in a photographer's studio

COUR DES LOGES 📖
6, rue du Bœuf
69005 Lyon
Tel. 04 72 77 44 44
www.courdesloges.com
contact@courdesloges.com

ROOMS AND RATES
247€ to 618€ per night
Breakfast: 25€
Open year round

Located in the Saint-Jean quarter at the heart of Vieux Lyon, the Cour des Loges is first and foremost an extraordinary architectural complex of 4 magnificent Renaissance structures (14th, 16th and 17th centuries), connected by the famous "traboules" (traditional passageways allowing inhabitants to pass from one building to another), and whose courtyards have been closed off to create a unique and sheltered space that is now occupied by the hotel's reception desk and gourmet restaurant.

Outdoor corridors lead to the rooms. On each floor, you'll find small sitting-rooms, and the view of the Italian loggia is magnificent. The rooms are all unique, but the most original are the photographer's room, entirely decorated with vintage photos, cameras, lamps and more, and the room inspired by an Italian opera box.

Surprisingly, an interior designer is part of the hotel staff and will sometimes lock himself in a room for several days to transform it, as he did for one of the private dining-rooms, endowed with a gorgeous and immense fireplace.

The hotel also possesses a café-grocery in a vaulted room. It offers affordable and quality cuisine.

PÉNICHE BARNUM

A B&B barge at the centre of Lyon

PÉNICHE BARNUM 102
3, quai Sarrail
69006 Lyon
Tel. 09 51 44 90 18
or 06 63 64 37 39
www.peniche-barnum.com
info@peniche-barnum.com

ROOMS AND RATES
2 cabins:
The Captain's quarters: 120€
(200€ for special events)
The Admiral's suite: 150€
(230€ for special events)
Folding bed for children
available upon request
(10€ for children 3 years
or older, free for children
younger than 3)
Breakfast: 10€
Open year round
Free supervised parking

Located at the centre of Lyon, the Barnum barge opened its B&B of two contemporary-style rooms, which one clearly doesn't expect to find on a barge, in 2008.

The view the barge offers of the quays of the Rhône River is gorgeous at any hour, even if the site is in high demand for the Festival of Lights on 8 December, the fireworks on 14 July, and New Year's Eve, when the reflection of the lights in the water clearly adds to the event's magic.

Tatiana, the owner, prepares a very good breakfast using fresh produce.

ÉCOTAGNES

Tree-houses and a teepee in the mountains

ÉCOTAGNES 103
Patrice Genand
74230 Les Villards-sur-Thônes
Tel. 06 70 02 10 14
www.ecotagnes.com
info@ecotagnes.com

ROOMS AND RATES
2 two-person
tree-houses
and 1 teepee
Summer (end of April to
15 October): 135€ per person,
130€ if you stay more
than 2 nights
Winter (15 October
to the end of April):
155€ per person,
150€ if you stay more
than 2 nights
Transport in a 4x4,
dinner, accommodation
and breakfast included

Patrice, a very dynamic man, invites guests to spend the night in a teepee or in two tree-houses near his chalet, just 60km from Geneva and 30km from Annecy.

The décor harmoniously fits the setting: wood, soft colours and large bay windows from which to enjoy nature and the view of the Aravis Range. In the summer, large terraces invite you to dine outdoors. A former technical adviser for Nicolas Hulot's "Ushuaïa" nature TV show, Patrice is a ski, paragliding, and hang-gliding instructor, as well as a helicopter pilot who is willing to share his hobbies with anyone looking for an adrenaline rush. He also offers the opportunity to follow courses in relaxation (Reiki energy-centring procedures for stress and pain) or to enjoy relaxing and energizing massages. In the summer, guests can go canyoning, hiking in the mountains, mountain climbing, mountain biking, horseback riding, take boat rides on Annecy Lake, or try the summer luge. In the winter, if you want to try something beyond the typical skiing activities, Patrice can take you sledding or on a visit to a frozen waterfall.

ANOTHER UNUSUAL HOTEL **NEARBY**

LE N'HÉRISSON 104

On a 35-acre property with a beautiful view of the Rhône River valley, Jocelyn and Nancy have installed different nomadic habitats. More than just an unusual type of accommodation, Jocelyn offers a veritable cultural experience of nomadic populations. When he welcomes his guests, and before dinner (a convivial table d'hôtes shared by all the guests), he takes great pleasure in imparting his knowledge.
- 2 yurts, 1 teepee, 1 Moroccan tent, 1 trapper's tent
- 69€ to 79€ per person, breakfast included.
  Dinner: 20€ to 26€ • 1 pony • Open April to October
- Le Molymard – 38150 **Saint-Romain-de-Surieu**
- Tel. 04 74 79 42 50
- elo@lenherisson.com • www.lenherisson.com

LA CABANE MAGIQUE

"The simplest pleasures are often the best!"

LA CABANE MAGIQUE **105**
Lionel Brun
349, Grande Rue
38660 Le Touvet
(postal address, not
that of the cabin)
Tel. 06 84 78 64 22
or 09 60 06 85 72
www.cabane-magique.fr
lionel.brun2@wanadoo.fr

ROOMS AND RATES
"Robinson" package:
accommodation,
breakfast
and "magic" cocktail: 145€
5-hour "Initiation to
relaxation massage"
for two,
accommodation and
breakfast: 530€
A la carte packages available
Open April to November

Built from salvaged wood and perched 2m above the ground, this magical small wooden cabin is at the heart of nature, at the foot of the Vercors massif.

Although the bedroom is small ($4m^2$) and there is no running water or electricity (just candlelight), the cabin is charming and its small terrace, where guests can enjoy breakfast, provides a pleasant view of the mountain.

Lionel and his girlfriend, who are relaxation therapy enthusiasts, also offer different types of relaxation and themed parties. Last, but not least, is what makes this cabin "magical": almost everything is possible, upon request – a bouquet of flowers for your arrival, a catered meal, or even fireworks.

GUEST COMMENTS
"You can't write about the cabin, you have to live it! A true pleasure."

A NIGHT IN AN IGLOO

Build your own igloo to sleep in!

A Night in an Igloo ⑩
Gilles Deloustal
Le Fuzier
38190 Laval
Tel. 06 09 89 80 04
or 04 76 68 74 08
http://pagesperso-orange.fr/
anne.tregloze//pas-a-pas/
gilles.deloustal@orange.fr

ROOMS AND RATES
250€ all-inclusive
(accommodation,
dinner, breakfast,
night in an igloo or cabin)
Snowshoe
and hiking-pole
rental included
Maximum of 12 participants

MEETING PLACE
Roughly 1h15
from Grenoble
(bus then taxi)
Belledonne Massif

Gilles, a professional mountain guide, offers a unique experience to anyone with an adventurous spirit: to build your own igloo to sleep in.

It all begins with a 3-hour snowshoe hike to reach the campsite. Then you have to choose the perfect place for your igloo and begin extracting snow bricks, with help from Gilles, of course, who will then guide you in constructing your igloo. Next, you'll melt snow to prepare dinner, as if you were on a true high mountain expedition.

For nervous, claustrophobic, or cold-sensitive guests (the temperature in the igloo fluctuates around 32°F, which is perfectly reasonable when sleeping in a "cold weather" sleeping-bag), Gilles has even prepared a solid shelter nearby where you can dine and sleep.

The meteorological conditions are crucial for the weekend's success. Indeed, it is impossible to build an igloo when there isn't enough snow or when the snow is too cold. You can also add snowshoe hikes, cross-country skiing (20km of marked trails) or downhill skiing (100km of ski-runs and 37 ski-lifts and the Les 7 Laux ski resort) to your weekend.

WEEKEND WITH A NIGHT
IN AN IGLOO ⑩
Bureau des guides et
accompagnateurs de l'Oisans
(Oisans Guide Office)
38520 Bourg d'Oisans
Florent Cancade: 06 79 97 91 62
f.cancade@orange.fr
Jean-Marc Giraud:
06 73 19 22 09
ethiqaventure@aliceadsl.fr
www.montagne-oisans.com

ROOMS AND RATES
5 to 8 participants – 100€
per person, includes dinner,
breakfast and lunch on Sunday
Snowshoes are provided
The ideal period is the end
of February and March
Belledonne Massif

For the past several years, the high mountain guides of Oisans have offered original weekend excursions: after a showshoe hike, you look for a place to sleep in the wild outdoors. After building the igloo, which takes about 2 hours, it's time to enjoy a cocktail and a Savoyard fondue meal in the snow! Although the temperature inside the igloo is 32°F (which doesn't pose a problem when you have a "cold weather" sleeping-bag), it is much colder outside (5°F–14°F) at an altitude of 1500m to 2000m. It is thus advisable to wait until sunrise before leaving the igloo!

THE ANCIENT CONVENT OF NOZIÈRES

The calm serenity of a convent

THE ANCIENT CONVENT OF NOZIÈRES ⑫
07270 Nozières
Tel. 04 75 07 69 21
http://anciencouventen.
nozieres.org/
anciencouvent@nozieres.org

ROOMS AND RATES
5 rooms
42€ per person
55€ for two people,
breakfast included
25€ for each
additional person
Children 16 and
younger: 15€,
free for children under 2
Table d'hôtes: 20€,
all-inclusive,
10€ for children,
free for children under 5
Open year round

Located at an altitude of nearly 1000m, the convent of Nozières was founded around 1760, at a time when many heeded the call to the sisterhood. This convent was home to the sisters of Saint Joseph, who taught the young girls of the region.

The convent's owners endeavoured to restore it while preserving the spirit and tranquility that reigned over the place when they first arrived. The bedrooms are decorated in a simple style, and although the walls are now coloured, the monastic ambiance is still present. One room has even been named after a mother superior: "Sister Marie-Ambroise's room".

A long corridor and pillared archways lead to the large sitting-room with its immense fireplace.

The table d'hôtes dinner is generous and convivial. The cuisine is prepared using regional produce.

GUEST COMMENTS

"There's a before and an after Nozières. The after seems rather dull."
"A warm welcome. A place of serenity that has preserved its spirit and its essence."

THE PHILOMÈNE CAMPSITE

Two caravans in the grounds of a château

LE CAMPEMENT PHILOMÈNE 109
Château d'Uzer
07110 Uzer
Tel. 04 75 36 89 21
www.chateau-uzer.com
château-uzer@wanadoo.fr

ROOMS AND RATES
3-night minimum stay:
110€ per night for 2 people,
breakfast not included
Table d'hôtes: 32€
Open from Easter to October

Located in the grounds of the Château d'Uzer, at the heart of the southern Ardèche region, the Philomène campsite is composed of two very comfortable caravans. The air-conditioned "night" caravan has a large bed, shower and toilet. The "day" caravan, which is linked to the other caravan by a shaded terrace, houses a kitchenette and a small sitting-room. The château's architecture has evolved over the centuries: a 13th-century tower, 15th-century vaults and staircase, and a wing dating from the 19th century. The owners have carried out its restoration in a harmoniously and discreet manner.

The grounds around the château are home to exuberant and tropical-like vegetation.

CAMPEMENT TAMANA

West Africa just steps from the Ardeche gorges

CAMPEMENT TAMANA 🔟
07700 Bidon
Reservations: 04 75 97 20
40 Monday to Friday, or 06
45 99 25 68 at weekends
www.campement-
tamana.com
Sonia@point-afrique.com

ROOMS AND RATES
6 habitats
50€ per night
for 2 people
20€ for each
additional person
10€ for children under 12,
free for children under 3
Breakfast basket: 5€
Senegalese or Mauritanian
dinners offered
some evenings
Solar showers and dry toilets
Open June to September

At the heart of the Ardeche region, the Tamana campsite is a stunning and glorious little corner of Africa.

The six huts, tents or charming straw huts, built on piles like loft storehouses, stand in the middle of wild natural surroundings. Inside the structures, you'll find cushions, mats and coffee tables but no electricity or mattresses, as is often the case in Africa.

Eating breakfast on the terrace opposite the garrigue is a true moment of pleasure. You'll discover West African specialties that take you on a journey of flavours: bissap, mango jam, ginger syrup (unusual for our western tastebuds), coconut jam and banana chips...

The word "Tamana" comes from Mali: "Ta" is a verb of movement meaning "go and come" and "mana" designates the person. "Tamana" can thus be translated to mean "he who goes and comes", like a traveller.

LE CHALET TOURNESOL

A house that rotates, like a sunflower

LE CHALET TOURNESOL ⑪
Isabelle Mascart
La Pierre
05800 Chauffayer
Tel. 04 92 21 40 98
www.lechalet.biz
contact@lechalet.biz

ROOMS AND RATES
4 B&B rooms
150€ per night
for 2 people,
on half-board
(dinner, room, breakfast,
access to the relaxation
and herb room),
reduced rates for stays
of 2 nights or more
Additional person:
20€ to 35€ on half-board
(free for children under 6)
100€ per night
for 2 people,
breakfast included
(10€ to 15€ for each
additional person)

In April, 2009, Isabelle had the excellent idea to open four guest-rooms in a stunning ecological house that she had built after having discovered the concept: the house is round, made entirely of wood, and rotates so as to capture the most sunlight possible.

Located in a small hamlet near the village of Chauffayer, at an altitude of 950m, the site provides a magnificent view of the mountains of the Écrins massif.

A 4-person jacuzzi can be found in the chalet's annex building.

AU FIL DES BRANCHES

Sleep in a hammock in the trees

AU FIL DES BRANCHES 🄓
Sylvie Zucco
Ancienne cure, Saint-Nicolas
05260 Saint-Jean-
Saint-Nicolas
Tel. 06 73 50 84 28
www.accompagnateurs-
champsaur.com
Sylvie.zucco@club-internet.fr

ROOMS AND RATES
60€ per person,
includes
half a day of tree-climbing,
accommodation,
and breakfast
40€ per person
for accommodation
and breakfast only
Family rate available
upon request
Children 6 and older allowed
Open May to mid-August,
depending on the weather
(if problems arise,
guests will be removed
to solid shelter)

The "Au Fil des Branches" association offers a rather unusual activity: after showing you how to climb trees, they simply give you the opportunity to spend the night there in a hammock hanging among the leaves.

Kept in balance by two rigid bars along their sides, the hammocks provide a comfortable night's sleep, almost as if you were in a bed. Some people even sleep all curled up! The only uncomfortable position is sleeping on your stomach because of the harness you must wear at all times to avoid the (very minimal) risk of falling in the middle of the night.

Five to a dozen people can be accommodated at a time. Unaccompanied people can join a group.

In the morning, a breakfast of fresh and organic produce is served.

THE NORDIC VILLAGE OF WILLIWAW

Spend the night in an igloo at an altitude of 2300m

THE NORDIC VILLAGER
OF WILLIWAW ⑬
Philippe Desmurger
05500 Saint-Laurent-du-Cros
Tel. 06 60 68 32 44
www.alpi-traineau.com
ph.desmurger@orange.fr

ROOMS AND RATES
Around 60€ per person
"Cold weather"
sleeping-bag rental: 5€
Open when
the weather allows

At an altitude of 2300m, in the slopes above the Orcières ski resort, Philippe offers to those who aren't overly sensitive to the cold (at night, the temperature can sometimes drop down to -4°F) the chance to experience the true adventure of sleeping in an igloo.

In the late afternoon, by ski lift or by snowshoe, guests climb to the Roche Rousse plateau, before starting on a hike to admire the sunset. If the party is small, a fondue dinner will be served in an igloo (if it's large, you'll dine in a mountainside restaurant – so try to keep your numbers small). Afterwards, it'll be time for a little stargazing (Philippe will help you recognize the constellations) before going to bed.

Contrary to what one might think, the igloos, which can hold a family of 4, have a temperature slightly above 32°F. Comfortably snuggled in a "cold weather" sleeping-bag, you'll likely sleep quite well!

The next day, you can do a little dog-sledding.

It's definitely not to be missed!

THE PERRET BUBBLE HOUSE

A round house, just like that of the Barbapapa family!

THE PERRET BUBBLE HOUSE ⑪
30580 Bouquet
Tel. 04 66 72 97 50
www.maisonbulle.com
contact@maisonbulle.com

ROOMS AND RATES
Self-catering
accommodation for 6 people
450€ to 600€ per week
depending on the season
House-cleaning available: 35€

Renowned French architect Auguste Perret (Le Corbusier was one of his students) was the first to grasp the importance of reinforced concrete. We owe numerous creations to him, including Le Havre's city centre, the Théâtre des Champs-Élysées or the Palais d'Iéna in Paris.

He also designed two bubble houses, built by Antti Lovag, which are privately owned. One of them has been turned into self-catering accommodation, which thus provides the privileged opportunity to spend some time in this architect's environment.

You can thus spend a week at the heart of the Gard region in this house where everything is round: the windows, walls, furniture, tables, chairs, and even the bed-frames!

MOULIN DE MAÎTRE CORNILLE

A mill opposite the Pont du Gard

MOULIN DE MAÎTRE CORNILLE 115
30210 Castillon du Gard
Tel. 04 66 57 04 27
www.
moulindemaitrecornille.com
moulindemaitrecornille@
wanadoo.fr

ROOMS AND RATES
3 rooms, 5 to 7 people
July and August:
1000€ to 1800€ per week,
depending on the period
June and September:
850€ per week
School holidays:
720€ per week
Other months:
550€ per week
Towels, sheets and
bathrobes provided
TV, swimming pool

The Moulin de Maître Cornille is an authentic 18th-century Provençal windmill that is still in working order. Located on a very peaceful property of 9,000m² in the middle of the garrigue, it is now home to three pleasant rooms that face the Pont du Gard, a Roman aqueduct bridge. A truly beautiful place, with a swimming pool.

DOMAINE DES 3 BORIES

Spend the night in a drystone hut

DOMAINE DES 3 BORIES 116
Eddy Le Compte
Col de Gordes – 84220 Gordes
Tel. 04 32 50 22 87
or 06 86 59 83 51
www.domainedes3bories.com
3bories@laposte.net

ROOMS AND RATES
3 rooms,
including 1 borie
95€ to 125€ per night
for 2 people in the low season
105€ to 140€ per night
for 2 people in the high season
30€ for each additional person
Breakfast included
(homemade jam)
Open March to October

ANOTHER UNUSUAL HOTEL
NEARBY

The Domaine des 3 Bories, located in the hills of Gordes, which is listed as one of France's most beautiful villages, is a 7.5-acre property that is fully enclosed by walls. A very beautiful overflow pool provides guests with an unrestricted view of the village and the Luberon, Alpilles and Monts de Vaucluse mountains.

Although all three rooms are charming, the one in the ancient *borie* is clearly the most interesting. These drystone huts used to serve as storage lofts, stables or seasonal residences for farmers in the 19th century. They are often restored and renovated into living space, as is the case here. The room remains deliciously cool on hot summer days.

LES BORIES DU SERRE 117

It's a veritable little hamlet of bories (nine in all) that Jean-Pierre Van der Pert has installed near Forcalquier, on quiet, tree-filled grounds surrounding a beautiful swimming pool. Although these structures have an undeniable charm when seen from the exterior, you must live in them for a while to learn all of their pleasures. They have been well designed, and seeing the dome from the inside creates a unique feeling. The amount of living space is surprising, as it is much larger than one would expect. A typical borie is composed of an entry/sitting-room that opens onto the kitchenette, 2 adjacent bedrooms and a mezzanine that provides extra sleeping space – ideal for a family.

- 3 borie groups accommodating 4 to 5 people each
- 650€ to 1390€ per week depending on the season. Weekend of 2/3 days (only during the off season): 290€ • Swimming pool
- Impasse des Restanques - 04300 **Forcalquier**
- Tel. 04 92 75 23 72
- Jean-Pierre Van der Pert • v.jeanpierre9@aliceadsl.fr
- www.boriesduserre.free.fr

LA CABANE DU PETIT LUBERON

A tree-house in the Luberon Mountains

LA CABANE DU PETIT LUBERON (118)
La Bastide du Bois bréant
501, chemin du
Puits-de-Grandaou
84660 Maubec-en-Luberon
Tel. 04 90 05 86 78
www.hotel-bastide-bois-breant.com
boisbreant@orange.fr

ROOMS AND RATES
100€ to 120€
per night,
2-night minimum,
breakfast included
Additional person: 30€,
breakfast included
Open March to October

Although Maubec may not be the prettiest village of the Luberon mountains, hidden behind its walls is a delightful little hotel, a former family residence, that has a charming tree-house set apart from its other rooms.

Built of red cider wood, the tree-house can comfortably accommodate a couple (and perhaps a child). It has a nice terrace where you can have breakfast (delivered in a basket), take a nap to the humming of cicadas, or gaze at the stars.

Since the tree-house doesn't have electricity, dynamo flashlights are left at your disposal. A bathroom reserved for the tree-house guests can be found next to the hotel.

There is also a very nice swimming pool and table d'hôtes dinner. The tree-house is ideally located for visiting the surrounding villages of Bonnieux, Oppède le Vieux, Lacoste and Gordes.

TROGLODYTE HOUSE

"For let: 60m² troglodyte house, exceptional, all comforts, double exposition, seasonal prices."

TROGLODYTE HOUSE 119
Mr and Mrs Ravel
22, quartier des Pénitents
13250 Saint-Chamas
Tel. 04 42 89 58 83
or 06 32 25 91 04
richard.ravel@wanadoo.fr

ROOMS AND RATES
Capacity:
4 people, but ideal
for a couple
with 2 children
270€ to 520€ per week,
depending on the season

Dug out of the cliffs of Saint-Chamas, the troglodyte house of Mr and Mrs Ravel invites you to spend a truly unique time on the banks of the Étang de Berre.

In fact, the house is a truly exceptional place. The apartment is a "run-through", which means that you enter by the hilly Delà quarter, which dominates the interior part of Saint-Chamas, and you come out on the terrace that overlooks the village's other quarter, the Pertuis, with a panoramic view of the Étang de Berre.

The view from the northern entrance through to the terrace to the south is really exceptional.

Those who have already stayed here have fallen in love with the place and have become regular guests. It is thus rather difficult to reserve. We suggest reserving as early as possible, or at the last minute if there has been a cancellation.

THE CARAVANS OF MAS DOU PASTRE

An air of bohemian elegance at Mas dou Pastre

THE CARAVANS OF MAS DOU PASTRE 120
Hotel Mas dou Pastre
Quartier Saint-Sixte
13810 Eygalières en Provence
Tel. 04 90 95 92 61
www.masdupastre.com
contact@masdupastre.com

ROOMS AND RATES
3 caravans
"La Gitane"
for 1 person: 80€
"La Manouche"
for 2 people: 125€
"La Voyageuse"
for 2 people: 150€
Breakfast: 15€ per person
Sweet and savoury snacks
for sale 12pm to 6pm

Albine and Maurice's old sheep farm ("pastre" is Provençal for "shepherd") has belonged to their family since 1750. When their parents died, they turned the rooms that used to store hay and sheep into bedrooms and decided to open the family farm to passing visitors.

Set in the prized countryside of the Alpilles mountains just 1km from the village of Eygalières, and 100m from the lovely Saint-Sixte chapel, Le Mas is a charming hotel surrounded by olive trees, cypress trees and lavender.

Three gypsy caravans have taken up residence at the back of the garden. The first caravan that they bought 25 years ago didn't survive the mistral's winds and storms, but they were able to save the furniture. Since these caravans were a common part of life at Le Mas (gypsies stopped at the farms to offer their services: reseating chairs, etc.), they were able to buy two others and recuperated a third, whose woodwork dates from 1920.

These colourful caravans add more than a touch of gaiety to the garden, which is also home to a heated swimming pool. The winter garden contains a whirlpool and a hammam offering chromotherapy (therapeutic use of colours).

A place to remember.

VILLA SANTA FE

A teepee camp and two vintage trailers

VILLA SANTA FE 🏷
Dominique and
Thierry Bertrand
1321, chemin des
Lonnes et du Velleron
13210 Saint-Rémy-
de-Provence
Tel. 09 75 94 70 37
or 06 10 48 01 63
www.lavillasantafe.com
contact@lavillasantafe.com

ROOMS AND RATES
3 teepees:
130€ to 200€ per night
for 2 people,
breakfast included
2 vintage 1960s trailers:
100€ to 120€
per night
for 2 people
Extra bed: 15€
Table d'hôtes: 38€,
cocktail included,
wine extra
Massages available
upon request
Outdoor jacuzzi

At a short distance from Saint-Rémy-de-Provence, you don't really expect to come across a camp of teepees, in a very ethnic-chic ambiance created by Dominique and Thierry.

In the summer, guests essentially sleep beneath the starry sky, and in the winter the teepee is covered with an insulating canvas so guests sleep in warmth.

The owners have also bought two 1950s/1960s trailers from a collector. Perfectly restored and decorated in a 1950s style, they have beautiful outdoor bathrooms, where old wine casks have been used to create the showers.

It is also possible to rent a red 1960s Cadillac cabriolet (with chauffeur) to visit the region while enjoying a glass of champagne.

In the evening, around a table d'hôtes, a generous meal is proposed.

A very pleasant place.

GUEST COMMENTS
"Coming to Villa Santa Fe is an extraordinary experience, with extraordinary people: a real pleasure!"

LES ATELIERS DE L'IMAGE

A tree-house where you can get away from it all

La cabane de l'hôtel
Les Ateliers de l'Image ⑫⑫
36, boulevard Victor Hugo
13210 Saint-Rémy-
de-Provence
Tel. 04 90 92 51 50
www.hotelphoto.com
info@hotelphoto.com

Rooms and rates
Rates for 2 people,
depending on the season:
Rooms: 165€ to 380€
Suites: 300€ to 550€
Tree-house suite:
300€ to 600€
Breakfast buffet: 19€
Open year round

Les Ateliers de l'Image hotel is a beautiful hotel that occupies an unusual building – the city's former music hall. Located on the circular boulevard that follows along the ancient ramparts of Saint-Rémy, it also possesses a lovely, tranquil garden with a magnificent view of the Alpilles mountains.

Among the rooms with a mountain view is a 45m² suite with a tree-house. A drawbridge leads to the tree-house, thus providing even more privacy – a perfect spot for lovers.

The interior design of the rooms is rather classical, as is the case for most of the other rooms as well.

The hotel regularly hosts photo exhibitions (photographs are displayed along the corridors and even in the rooms), and organizes photography classes, film shows and jazz concerts.

Also at the hotel you'll find a restaurant, a sushi bar, massages and reflexology sessions.

Great tranquility at the heart of a "jet-set" village.

THE BOATEL

A true boat-hotel

THE BOATEL 🔢
Pont Van Gogh
13200 Arles
Tel. 06 08 60 53 24
www.leboatel.com
leboatel@leboatel.com

ROOMS AND RATES:
7 cabins with
bathroom and wi-fi
1 April to 30 September:
2-porthole cabin 110€
1-porthole cabin 90€
1 October to 31 March:
100€ and 80€
Breakfast: 9€
Weekend Special:
130€ for 2 people,
including 2 meals
(drinks not included),
room and 2 breakfasts;
or 150€ for 2 people,
including 2 cabaret dinners
(drinks not included),
room and 2 breakfasts
Jacuzzi

The Boatel, a 50m-long boat-hotel, is an old 1958 cargo barge that Richard and Pernette bought in Belgium. Much longer than typical Freycinet-style barges, it had to be cut in two so it could pass through the region's locks and be brought to Arles.

Today, 7 cabins decorated in a clean, contemporary style are open to visitors.

Music concerts are held here regularly.

THE GUARDIAN HOUSE

Sleep in a real Camargue guardian house

THE GUARDIAN HOUSE 124
Annick and Patrick Biermann
13, avenue Riquette Aubanel
13460 Les Saintes-
Maries-de-la-Mer
Tel. 04 90 49 67 67
or 06 20 78 25 35
www.maisondegardian.com
pbie@wanadoo.fr

ROOMS AND RATES
700€ to 1180€
per week depending on
the season and the number
of people (maximum 6)
Garden and enclosed parking
2 double rooms
and a mezzanine
with two single beds
Open year round

Only a few, rare authentic guardian houses, once home to the famous horse-herders of the Camargue, are available as seasonal rentals. The Biermann family's "cabin" is ideally located facing the Saintes beach, just a 3-minute walk from the centre of Saintes-Maries-de-la-Mer.

Another advantage: the strip of land leading to the beach to the south and to the Étang des Launes to the north, on which the cabin stands, is part of the "Pont du mort" neighbourhood, which was reserved only for guardian houses in the 1950s, to preserve the village's traditional aspect at a time when new buildings were springing up everywhere. The Étang de Launes is home to pink flamingoes, wild ducks, herons, and wild bulls at night – so watch out!

The guardian house

A symbol of Camargue-style architecture, the guardian house is shaped like an upside-down boat, with the round part (apse) facing the dominant wind (the mistral) and bearing the inclined cross. The main façade is a windowless, whitewashed gable wall topped by a very steep reed roof. Originally, this type of makeshift residence was made for horse-herders who moved from pasture to pasture with their herds. Easy to build, and made primarily of reeds tied up in bundles called "manons", these cabins protected them from the rain and wind, which, in the Camargue, could be extremely violent. A rope strung from the apse to a stake planted in the ground helped solidify the structure. The apse, which was relatively high, served as a stable. Today, these cabins have become "thatched cottages" and are sometimes quite luxurious: windows have been added, the room beneath the apse has been turned into a spacious living-room, and bedrooms have been added upstairs.

Other guardian houses for let: Jean-Pierre and Sophie Gonet, www.les-cabanes-de-gardian.camargue.fr

THE LE CORBUSIER HOTEL

A unique way to spend the night in a Le Corbusier building

THE LE CORBUSIER HOTEL ⑫⑤
Cité Radieuse
280, boulevard Michelet
13008 Marseille
Tel. 04 91 16 78 00
www.hotellecorbusier.com
contact@
hotellecorbusier.com

ROOMS AND RATES
21 rooms
Rates ranging
from 65€
for a 16m² "cabin"
room with terrace,
sparse but both comfortable
and welcoming,
for those on a small budget,
for "Corbu" aficionados,
95€ for a 32m² studio
with a park view
with 2 balconies
and up to 4 single beds
The large, 32m² rooms
with ocean view are at 118€
Two 32m² studios
with ocean view,
114€ and 125€
with a nice terrace
and original kitchenette (just
for viewing – not to be used!)
Mini-suite with
ocean view: 125€
Breakfast: 9€
Extra bed: 15€

Almost as famous as the nearby velodrome stadium, Le Corbusier's "Cité Radieuse" (Radiant City), classed as a historic monument, possesses a hotel on the third floor. Unknown to most of Marseille's residents, it was taken over in 2003 by a couple of architecture enthusiasts who redecorated it in the spirit of the period, by reintegrating some of the original furniture and light fixtures and having others reproduced (with the authorization of Charlotte Perriand, who was part of the team). Although the result is true to the original, many clients don't necessarily appreciate the "master's" architecture: the corridors are long, dark and sinister, and the rather sparse décor doesn't really give it the feeling of an up-scale hotel. Situated outside of Marseille's city centre, the site will delight fans of Le Corbusier most of all.

The rest of the building, which is a veritable village in and of itself, is also open to the hotel's clients: a 40-seat cinema, fitness room and sauna, jogging lanes, children's wading pool, and a concert hall on the roof terrace.

From the restaurant's terrace (where breakfast is served), you have a glorious view of the sea and the Frioul Islands.

THE CHÂTEAU DES CREISSAUDS TREE-HOUSE

A cabin in the trees for lovers

THE CHÂTEAU DES CREISSAUDS TREE-HOUSE ⑫⑥
Clos Rufisque
13400 Aubagne
Tel. 04 91 24 84 45
www.maisonperchee.com
contact@
chateaudescreissauds.com

ROOMS AND RATES
1 tree-house
70€ to 100€ per night
for 2 people,
depending on the season
(we suggest reserving
several months in advance)
Sleeping arrangements
for young children ages
3 or older possible
Swimming pool,
tennis court,
squash court
Open year round

The Château des Creissauds is a lovely 19th-century residence on a 200-acre property planted with over 100-year-old trees. Standing 6m above ground, the wooden tree-house at the top of a plane tree is a veritable lover's cabin: 360° view, bedroom, living-room, kitchenette, bathroom, and a terrace where you can have breakfast.

The Dans les Arbres restaurant, which stands in a tree 4m above the ground, is open from the end of May to the beginning of September, and offers the same ambience.

LA ROYANTE

A bathroom with a view of the chapel...

LA ROYANTE **127**
Xenia and Bernard Saltiel
Chemin de la Royante
13400 Aubagne
Tel. 04 42 03 83 42
www.laroyante.com
xbsaltiel@aol.com

ROOMS AND RATES
4 rooms
129€ to 159€
for 2 people depending
on the room and the season
Breakfast included
Open year round

Located 5 minutes from the centre of Aubagne, La Royante is a truly beautiful country house surrounded by immense grounds that include an overflow pool. The former summer residence of the bishops of Marseille, the property possesses an imposing chapel that was consecrated by Pope Pius IX. Dedicated to the four evangelists and embellished with lovely stained-glass windows, the chapel once had a sacristy that is now occupied by one of the four guestrooms at La Royante. Furnished in period style, each room has its own unique atmosphere.

The most astonishing room is perhaps the Saint-Thomas room, which is connected to the chapel by its bathroom; a stained-glass window depicting the apostle separates the two. It is thus perfect for bathing beneath the watchful eyes of Saint Thomas.

Finally, as comments left in the guest book indicate, it would seem that the site is filled with unique vibrations. For those who would like to have their local diviner analyze the site's telluric impact from a distance, its GPS co-ordinates are: 5° 33' 02" East / 43° 18' 06" North.

THE TUANI CONVENT

Sleep in a former convent

THE TUANI CONVENT
20226 Costa
Belgodere Haute-Corse
Tel. 04 95 61 07 43
or 06 21 76 75 43
www.couventdetuani.com
fauconnier.denis2@
wanadoo.fr

ROOMS AND RATES
Rates for the entire
convent (16 rooms)
(not including the church):
2450€ per week or 4500€
for 2 weeks (mid-May,
June and September);
2800€ per week or
5200€ for 2 weeks
(first 2 weeks of July and
the last 2 weeks of August);
3500€ per week or 6600€
for 2 weeks
(last 2 weeks of July and
first 2 weeks of August)
Capacity: 20 people
Open May to October
A 15-minute drive
from the beach

If you have around 20 people in your group, the Tuani Convent would be a unique way to discover the Balagne region.

At an altitude of 400m, the convent is a former monastery founded in 1494 that is classed as a historic monument. Purchased from Catherine Deneuve, who bought it in 1969 after its closure (too few monks remained), the site has retained the isolation and tranquility that gives it its charm.

When it is not rented out, the current owners live in the convent, maintaining it and renovating it when necessary. Your stay will probably help fund their church restoration project.

An oil mill located along a river, in the middle of a field of olive trees, is also available for let (capacity: 6 people).

THE CHÂTEAU VALMER TREE-HOUSE

A tree-house in a vineyard

**THE CHÂTEAU VALMER
TREE-HOUSE** ⓫
Hôtel Château Valmer
Route de Gigaro
83420 La Croix-Valmer
Tel. +33 (0)4 94 55 15 15
www.chateauvalmer.com
info@chateauvalmer.com

ROOMS AND RATES
355€ to 490€
for 2 people,
depending on the season
Another tree-house
for 4 people is also
available: 480€ to 690€
The main hotel's spa
is open to all clients
Open year round

Standing 6m above ground in the branches of an immense 100-year-old oak tree on the Château Valmer estate, the tree-house is a romantic refuge of overwhelming charm. Isolated from the rest of the château in the middle of a vineyard that covers the majority of this 19th-century estate, the tree-house is probably the most beautiful of its kind in France. Only the price might disappoint some. In the summer, you can have a delicious breakfast brought right to the bedroom door. Although you can't see the ocean from the tree-house, it is nevertheless nearby, barely 200m away, at the end of a gorgeous pathway lined by 100-year-old trees.

The beach itself is probably one of the most beautiful and wild beaches along the French Riviera. A few rare buildings, including the annex of the Château Valmer, with a swimming pool and restaurant, make this site a very pleasant place.

On the left, after a second beach with more buildings, a pathway begins along the coast which, after a few hours of walking, will lead you to the Saint-Tropez peninsula. Bought in 1949 by the parents of the current owners, Château Valmer was progressively turned into a 4-star hotel with 42-two rooms, a restaurant, spa, sauna and hammam.

HI HOTEL

A futuristic hotel

HI HOTEL
3, avenue des Fleurs
06000 Nice
Tel. 04 97 07 26 26
www.hi-hotel.net
hi@hi-hotel.net

ROOMS AND RATES
38 rooms
219€ to 750€ per night
Open year round

Designed by Matali Crasset in 1993 with the idea of improving the standards of luxury hotels, the Hi Hotel is a hotel unlike any other. Designer and futurist, it will delight those who like to be surprised.

The bedroom and the bathroom aren't always separated, which clearly limits one's privacy. Another drawback is that the hotel doesn't have direct access to the beach, which isn't very far away, however.

GUEST COMMENTS

"No other hotel is like this one. It's a unique place."
"A perfect welcome in this spaceship."

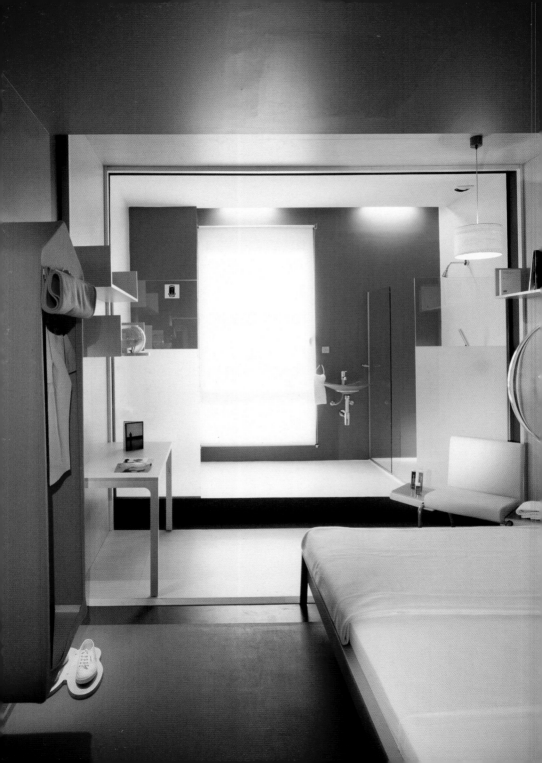

HOTEL WINDSOR

"Each room is a work of art"

HÔTEL WINDSOR ⓫
11, rue Dalpozzo
06000 Nice
Tel. 04 93 88 59 35
www.hotelwindsornice.com
contact@
hotelwindsornice.com

ROOMS AND RATES
90€ to 155€ in low season;
120€ to 175€ in high season
Breakfast: 12€
Half-board: 34€
Extra bed: 20€
Swimming pool,
relaxation centre
Sauna, hammam and
massages (supplement),
fitness room
Wi-fi
Bar and restaurant
Open year round

Besides being a unique hotel, Hotel Windsor is simply one of the best hotels in Nice: a charming welcome, a beach just a 2-minute walk away, a swimming pool in the garden. And that, of course, is without mentioning that a majority of the rooms have been decorated by artists.

Although the most spectacular room is probably the one Parmiggiani designed as a golden cube with a striped, white bed, other rooms are also interesting.

Those designed by Ben and Joël Ducorroy outshine by their humour and allusions. Charlemagne Palestine, Jean-Pierre Bertrand, Philippe Perrin, François Morellet, Glen Baxter and many others have also given free reign to their imagination. Room 238, designed by Varini, has a unique feature: the graphic coherence of the red line that runs throughout the room, entry and bathroom can only be fully appreciated from one specific spot in the room.

Plan to spend some time exploring to discover all the hotel's secrets.

ACKNOWLEDGEMENTS

Antoine Arnous, Irène Arrouch, Nicole Arquier,
Nathalie Auguste, Hubert Avatanéo, Nicolas Barsotti,
Isabelle and Patrice Bellon, Sébastien Bénistant,
Maud Berezig, Marc Berthet, Dominique and Thierry
Bertrand, Annick and Patrick Biermann, Jean-Luc Blain,
Marcel Bodéré, Vincent Bonnot, Marianne Borthayre
and Jean Luc Mathias, Yves and Michèle Bouquet,
Philippe and Nelly Bouret, Jacques Boy, Lionel Brun,
Elisabeth Bruno, Frédérique and Jacques Buffière,
Florent Candade, Olivier Capiau, Capucine, Augustin
and Philippine, Cloé Castellas, Francis Caussieu,
Agnès Chaouche, Anne du Chayla, Muriel and Eric
Chevalier, Claire Cousin, Violaine Decré, Catherine
Degardin, Robin Delaporte, Gilles Deloustal, Francette
Desmette, Philippe Desmurger, Isabelle Desrues, Diane
des Diguères, Tibo Dhermy, Steve Dobson, Hugues
Droulers, Denis Duchêne, Camille Dugas, Michèle
Duvivier, Jeroen Elkhuizen, Paulette Esnard, Sonia
Esseghir, Yann Falquerho, Eliane Fau, Denis and Marie-
Antoinette Fauconnier, Florence, Isabelle Fremont,
Anne-Marie and Charles Frénéa, Loïc Gallerand, Annie
Gay, Patrice Genand, Dominique and Alban Gérardin,
Jean-Pierre Gonet, Philippe Goninet, Laure and Bruno
Goude, Sheïla and Ursus Gruninger, Jean-François
Guenin, Romaine Guérin, Hervé Guichet and Lucien
Cassat, Karine Guihard, Florence Hale, Jocelyn and
Nancy Hernandez, Bertrand Hodicq, Nicolas Hodicq,
Anne Hourman, Frédéric Jean, Frédéric and Sue
Jeanniot, Daniel Jegat, Guillaume Jonglez, Thomas
Jonglez, Chantal de Knyff, Olivier and Armelle de la
Blanchardière and their children, Dorothée Laot, Eddy
le Compte, Jean-François and Chantal Lecomte, Marie
and Stéphane Lefaucheux, Serge Lemonnier, Adriaan
Lokman and Liesbeth Konink, Marie and Mickaël
of the Boudoir de Serendipity, Myriam and Arno le
Masle, Danièle Magne, Karine Mahéo, Régis Maillard,
Isabelle Mascart, Hervé de Mazerac, Bernard Maymou
and Olivia Gemain, Patricia Meneguen, the Monnet
family, Bertrand Monthuir, Bernard Montimart, Maria
Nasr, Bernard Noé, Alain Noualhat, Stéphanie Olivier,
Antoine and Sandrine Paris, Pascaline and Pascal Patin,
Perry and Coline de Belrpayre, Friedrich Pfeffer, the
Piot family, and especially LO-renzo, Richard and
Sylvette Ravel, Philippe and Michèle Régis, Christian
and Ghislaine de Régloix, Guillaume Reynaud, Numa
Rocchietta, Albine and Maurice Roumanille, Séverine
Rudigoz, Xenia and Bernard Saltiel, Mr and Mrs
Sampietro, Cathy and Alain Sarrazin, Benoît Sautillet,
Audrey Schlagbauer, Florian Soulié, Claire Stickland and
Ivan Payonne, Tatiana of the Péniche Barnum, Mr and
Mrs Jacques Thénard, Bruno Tourmen, Linda Tribet,
Emilie Trinel, Florence Vacher, Hélène Vacher, Jean-
Marc Valverde, Aude and Kees van Beek, Jean-Pierre
van der Pert, Gwenaëlle Versmée, Fabrice Villembits,
Caroline and Philippe Wadoux, Guillaume Wibaux,
Bertrand Wilmart, Sylvie Zucco.

The Tourist Offices and Departmental Tourism
Committees, and notably that of Orcières, Gîtes de
France, the Demeures de Thiérache, all those who
helped us develop this book as well as all the hotel and
B&B owners for their hospitality.

Maps: Jean-Baptiste Neny
Design: Roland Deloi
Lay-out: Stéphanie Benoit
English translation: Kimberly Bess
Editing: Kenneth Burnley